When God Comes Near

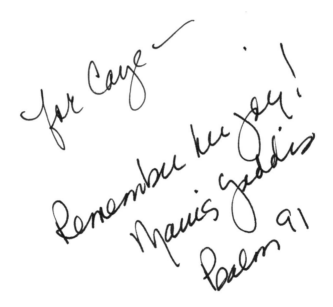

for Gaye —
Remember her Joy!
Mavis Geddis
Psalm 91

❦   *In Memory of*   ❧

Megan McQueen Gaddis

August 10, 1981
to
September 12, 2008

When God Comes Near

Waiting in the miracle of His presence

Marcia Gaddis

Longbranch Press

ATLANTA

MMX

This book is printed on acid-free paper which conforms to the American National Standard Z39.48.1984 Permanence of Paper for Printed Library Materials. Paper that conforms to this standard's requirements for pH, alkaline reserve, and freedom from groundwood is anticipated to last several hundred years without significant deterioration under normal library use and storage conditions.

Published by Longbranch Press, 780 Registry Lane, Atlanta, Georgia USA 30342
Manufactured in the United States of America

First Edition
ISBN 978-0-578-06367-6

To my family:

Mike, Megan, Owen and Blair.

Death has not ripped us apart,

but love is holding us close.

I will always love you.

Acknowledgements

Many books bear the name of one author, but it takes many hands to make it become a reality.

To the thousands who responded to the journaling from the early days of Megan's illness, you gave me strength to write each week. As I struggled to give credence to what I could not believe, a story began—one that I would have preferred not to experience or write about—one that became a mysterious journey of faith.

To Megan's Angels who prayed every Tuesday for sixteen months at my dear friend Bonnie Copeland's home. You came together to sit in silence or to pray. And as the weeks turned to months, you remained faithful. It became a time of waiting on God—feeling His presence and trusting Him.

To faithful friends who came weekly to sit with Megan—Bonnie, Kathleen, Toni, Carol, Lu, and Connie. You each brought your gifts of love and support. The hundreds of others who wrote weekly, or delivered tokens of love, or sent messages through the web site were examples of how the Holy Spirit prompts us to reach out.

To Megan's many friends who stayed close throughout the journey and still hold us close today. You have included us in your life events and continue to remember Megan in ways that surprise us and bring joy to our hearts.

To the Book Angels—too many to name. You have prayed every week beginning in January of 2010 for the progress of this book you now hold in your hand.

To my sisters and brother, and to my extended family who supported us from afar. Your solid faith and fervent prayers kept me grounded. I am so thankful to have had parents and grandparents who loved the Lord and lived out that love.

To Bob and Myra Marsh and to Betsy Lunz. Your spiritual guidance and faithful presence permeated our home and our hearts with compassion, trust, and confidence in the resurrected life.

To Greg Hyde, former teacher of Megan, who did the hard job of initial editing. You generously helped me to clear my vague thoughts and pushed me to go a little further in my painful memories. You even shed a tear or two with me and inspired me to read more great literature.

To Mary Sommers who did the final editing. Not knowing me, you weren't shy about correcting my mistakes and helped me to understand why we do the things we do. I am so thankful there are people like you who can make me look like a real writer.

To David Laufer, my publisher, who was there from the beginning, quietly observing and supporting. You stepped forward to actually make the book a reality. You worked with your heart as well as your head. You are an extremely creative and thoughtful man.

And to all who will read this book...thank you for reading a story that God inspired. I work daily to be grateful for the privilege of sharing it.

Introduction

The first butterfly of summer just appeared in my garden reminding me of my daughter Megan. As she neared the end of her life, I called her my butterfly while I watched her eyes flutter as she drifted in and out of sleep. As the summer turned to fall and the butterflies left the garden, Megan left with them on September 12, 2008.

It's like a nightmare—cruel beyond belief that my daughter, a 27-year-old, seemingly healthy woman, could be diagnosed with one of the rarest diseases known in the world, Creutzfeldt-Jakob disease—a disease that affects only 1 in 100,000,000 young people (16-34 years of age), a disease for which there is no known cure or treatment, a disease that destroys brain cells in a relatively short period of time, a disease that is fatal.

As much as I have written about this journey of suffering, hope, and mysterious transformation, I still often find it hard to believe this really happened to us—our beautiful family of five. And now Mike, Owen, Blair, and I try to live each day without her. Some days are better than others. We try to act normally when everything is different and will always be different. It is hard and I wonder if we will ever feel like a family again. I pray and trust that we will.

And yet I know it was an experience so deep and so mysterious that it will never leave the core of our hearts and minds and never cease to teach us about God's love. It was a cross that was almost too hard to bear. It was a cross that we were handed and we accepted—unwillingly, but obediently. Someone once said that if everyone's crosses were piled up and we could choose one, we would still choose our own. I believe that. You see, God's presence moved into our home in a mysteriously powerful way, giving us comfort and courage and grace to face each day as Megan, our butterfly, slipped from our lives and into the full presence of God.

I share a story that God wrote for us as He drew near to us in our sorrow and pain. As I cared for her the words came—sometimes through prayer, sometimes through disbelieving tears and anger, disappointment and pleading, but always out of obedience and with great hope. The journaling seemed to give me energy for the journey. As the news of Megan's diagnosis spread, many who never knew her walked the journey with us, mourned her death, and celebrated her life. I believe it is a story in which Megan, if handed it to read, would be humbled and give God all the honor and praise. And that is my intention as I offer this true story of faith in the midst of my darkest hours.

You might have unspeakable circumstances in your life. No matter what they are, God will come near. If you look closely you will find Him in surprising ways. I did.

Marcia Gaddis
Spring 2010

Foreword

It was at the end of the day, and I was annoyed to be walking into the hospital instead of going home. The inpatient neurology team had asked me to offer input on a young patient who had been admitted with puzzling symptoms. After having heard a very brief summary, a small skeptical voice in my head began whispering, "It's 16-34 disease..." In the sometimes patronizing and often arrogant world of medicine, we tend to believe that neurological symptoms (such as paralysis, vision loss, seizures, and a host of other creative possibilities) that defy our understanding are manifestations of neuroses. In our still male-dominated culture, we are particularly likely to draw that conclusion when the one with the audacity to challenge our diagnostic acumen is a female. When she is an otherwise healthy young woman, often between the ages of 16-34, the level of suspicion goes off the scales.

My cynicism left me quickly upon meeting Megan and her parents. There was nothing to suggest a hint of anything other than what this appeared to be—a young woman experiencing a devastating and rapid deterioration in her higher brain functions. Megan was open and friendly, and she did her very best to cooperate with everything I asked of her. There were no inconsistencies in her examination, and there were physical findings that would be almost impossible to feign. Her parents were obviously anxious, but they were no less open with me. They had already seen many doctors, and it was clear that they had encountered personal questions probing into Megan's life and potential sources of stress or psychological trauma. They answered honestly and thoroughly. There was no defensiveness. There was no hesitation. There was only the fear of parents who knew that their daughter was ill and that her illness was serious.

Before I left the hospital that night I knew we were in trouble. My note in Megan's chart listed potential explanations for her illness, and the three most likely diagnoses were all rare and all bad: central nervous system vasculitis, paraneoplastic limbic encephalitis, and Creutzfeldt-Jakob disease. Test results already tended to argue against the first two possibilities, and from a clinical standpoint Megan's illness fit best with a diagnosis of Creutzfeldt-Jakob disease. There was just one major inconsistency. Twenty-six-year-olds don't get Creutzfeldt-Jakob disease. It is an illness that typically occurs in the sixth or seventh decade of life. Over the past 15 years I have seen perhaps 50 or 60 patients with CJD, and none were close to Megan's age. That may not seem like a very big number, but consider that annually CJD strikes one individual out of a million. In 2007, the world's population was around 6.5 billion souls. In 2007, there may have been about 6500 cases of CJD worldwide. In 2007, I think Megan was perhaps the youngest person with CJD anywhere on the planet.

As a neurologist and as a scientist, I could not help but wonder at Megan, the unbelievable medical oddity. As a father with a daughter, I could not escape the absolute horror of the tragedy. As a human being who questions meaning and faith, I continue to struggle with what Megan forced me to contemplate. I viewed glimpses of the Megan that I never knew through conversations with Marcia and Mike and the sharing of friends and family at her memorial service. Through her writing Marcia has allowed me to know her daughter a little better, and I am very grateful. This book is a chronicle of a journey that should never have been, and it is a path of healing for a wound that no parent should suffer. I pray for its success.

James J. Lah, MD, PhD
Alice and Roy Richards Professor of Neurology
Director, Emory Cognitive Neurology Program
Atlanta, Georgia

Contents

When God Comes Near

Chapter One **Forever**

Death *teaches us that what we love* about a person is not her smile or touch, but that which comes from deep within the soul. I began to understand that as we watched Megan's spirit leave her body. As death consumed her, she changed. The light in her eyes dimmed. She became a breathing skeleton. Her face became expressionless and pale. No longer would we see those raised, perfectly shaped eyebrows and that knowing sparkle in her big brown eyes. Her body temperature began to cool and her skin felt dry and rough. She became almost unrecognizable. Megan—our daughter, sister, and friend—was no longer there.

As her spirit transitioned from her body to the presence of God, the life we knew and loved for 27 short years had gone. On the morning of September 12, 2008, I suggested to our nurse that she dress Megan in traveling clothes, simply thinking death could come any minute. While she was drying and brushing Megan's hair, we noticed two tears running down Megan's cheeks. Surprised by this form of tender communication, I whispered, choking back my own tears, "Felicia, I think she's telling us good-bye."

That night, while we stepped away from her bedside for a few minutes, Megan's spirit flew away to God. Free at last, she took flight to new life and left in her bed the disease that had held her captive for sixteen months. Hospice came within minutes. Megan's body was taken to Emory where her brain and spinal column were donated for research. Calls were made, family and friends gathered, and the carefully prepared obituary was sent out.

Somehow, unknowingly, we prepare for the end of life. I often hear stories about people being prepared for death—making that unplanned visit or phone call days or weeks before seeing someone for the last time. I, too, was being prepared. In the last two weeks of Megan's life, my journal writing, hereafter in *italics*, reflected her imminent death.

•◦ SEPTEMBER 1, 2008 *It is Finished*

Before Megan entered the hospital in 2007, we returned to her classroom to give her students what Megan called her "summer gift" and to celebrate their first year in school. Megan's assistant told her that one of her children wanted to pray with her—his name was Gabriel. We went to a private room where Megan sat with Gabriel by her side, holding her hand. With his left hand, he reached up and put his little hand on her forehead and bowed his head. We followed his lead and he prayed his prayer in hushed Spanish. When he said "Amen" he raised his head, solemnly looked at Megan and said, "It is finished."

I have thought about this event often, marveling at the love of a child, his angelic name, his privately offered prayer, his last sentence in English. The angel Gabriel appeared in the Bible at times of importance—Daniel's dream, as well as Joseph, Mary, and Elizabeth's news of the birth of Jesus and John. For Gabriel to pray with Megan will always be mysterious to me. That he would solemnly conclude with the same statement Jesus uttered before he died, "It is finished"—well, it takes my breath away. Had we too been sent the angel Gabriel to warn us, to prepare us for what was to come?

It is indeed almost finished—Megan has been sleeping peacefully for a week. She has had little food or water. Her sister Blair and brother Owen have said their good-byes. Affectionately known now as Dr.

Feelgood, my husband Mike, has said good-bye. And as I am slowly saying my own, I realize Megan was driven with a passion that moved her quickly through her life's work and I seem to be left with trying to make sense of it all.

We are grateful to our Hospice nurses who come daily to tenderly care for Megan. We know that having her at home has been the right choice and a gift to all of us. She has brought us much joy and comfort through this year—even her limitations could not stop her from shining light and love to all who have been with her. I only pray that she has felt our love in return.

Maybe that is why God allowed her to remain with us for as long as He did. Maybe that is why God controlled the ravaging effects of Creutzfeldt-Jakob disease in her, a disease that, according to Megan's doctor, affects only one in 100,000,000 young people. Through it all, she was able to offer love and hope to many. Maybe that is why she did not lose her eyesight or experience other harsh symptoms of the disease, so that many would want to hug her and hold her hand and talk to her, as if they hoped she might understand their love for her.

One night, Mike stroked her hair and said, "She is out of this world." Yes, she is, but I can still see the rise and fall of her breathing as I write. And the words of Jesus give me comfort, "Take heart! I have overcome even the world."

On September 10, 2008, two days before her death, I was thinking about what might have been, and about her friend who was getting married.

SEPTEMBER 10, 2008

Standing in my kitchen a friend looked down on the counter where in a small pile were one okra pod, five cherry tomatoes, and one small yellow pepper. "So, is this the harvest?" she said, trying not to laugh. I confessed it was. After all my talk about planting a garden and harvesting lush vegetables, we have had few homegrown feasts at our table.

But we have had greater feasts celebrating love and friendship this year. When I say the 23rd Psalm to Megan, it speaks of God preparing a table for us in the presence of our enemies, and yes, He has provided us with rich love through this fight with disease, our enemy. But the Bible speaks of another feast in the book of Matthew. There is a parable about the bridesmaids getting ready for a wedding feast. Not all of them were ready and when the bridegroom came, those who were ready went in with him to the marriage feast, and the door was locked. The others were left out.

Of course, I am thinking about Megan's friend who is getting married this Saturday. The preparations have been made. The bride and bridesmaids are ready. The groom will greet his chosen bride and the wedding celebration will begin. Megan would have been at that wedding, celebrating. Instead, she is ready and waiting for an eternal feast in Heaven with God, her Bridegroom, whose affection for her is beyond measure.

Like Megan, none of us know when we will be called to go into the feast. But we can be getting ready. We can take time to commune lovingly with the Lord. Jesus said in John 14:3 "When everything is ready, I will come and get you, so that you will always be with me where I am."

I can see her now being welcomed into this feast with our Lord. I see her radiant in the love of Christ, beautiful beyond description, and safely home.

Having that picture in my mind enabled me to face the moment of her death. But the moment of her death was only between Megan and God. We were not at her bedside. It must have been peaceful and dignified for Megan. She slipped quietly through the door, probably smiling at her new freedom. I laid my head on her perfectly still body and thanked God for taking her safely home at last. We were calm and quiet as we made the phone calls that so many were expecting. To this day, I can't remember making those calls. I watched my friends take over the kitchen with authority. Flowers, along with relatives, began to arrive. Voices were hushed and controlled as we made the final arrangements with the church. We sent the obituary to the Atlanta Journal Constitution. On the Monday of the service, Mike and I picked up Megan's ashes and on the way to the church we laughed with Blair and Owen about buckling Megan up for safety. Laughter was good medicine in the midst of grief. And as we went through those days of great sorrow, reflecting on the events before and after her immediate death, a beautiful theme began to weave through the words I wrote.

ᴏ‿ SEPTEMBER 16, 2008 *Forever*
Tuesday, one day after Megan's Memorial Service…
We are tired, but energized;
   sad, but joyful;
    relieved, yet lonely;
      wanting quiet, but finding it much too still;
       death so final and yet, eternity forever.
I believe it was a service that pleased our Lord, honoring Megan's life, the gift we were allowed to love in person for 27 years. The message of the Christian faith was presented with clarity, conviction, and extreme grace. The friends who spoke, sang, performed, and prayed poured out their hearts to a sanctuary overflowing with family and friends who have been touched by Megan and her faithful journey to Heaven.
I could feel her presence worshipping with us and giving Jesus Christ the honor and glory which He so greatly deserves. I could hear her singing her favorite hymn "Be Thou My Vision" along with the soloist. I could hear her laughing about the friendship stories told by her best friends, Lindsay and Kate; I could see her admiring Betty Ashton play the harp—she said she would have her play at her wedding one day. I could see her taking a note or two in the margins of her Bible as she listened attentively to Bob, Betsy, Manfred, and Bill. And I could see her somewhere high above the clouds, worshipping the God that she loved and served.

7

As we have cried and laughed and remembered the day, a beautiful theme has woven itself through the course of events. Three repetitions clearly affirmed the message of the Gospel that was delivered. When Betsy spoke lovingly of visiting with Megan through her illness, she told about saying the Lord's Prayer with Megan when she could still talk. Betsy asked Megan to end the prayer by saying "Amen." But Megan was ahead of her and when they got to "For Thine is the kingdom and the power and the glory" Megan quickly said "Forever." And when Lindsay was at the end of her remarks, she closed with "Eternity is forever." Finally, the closing words in the Benediction Response was "Bless and keep you forever."

This morning when I opened my devotional book to September 16, the verse for me from Isaiah was, "The fruit of righteousness will be peace, the effect of righteousness will be quietness and confidence forever."

My friends, we have peace and quietness and confidence because God's Spirit has been among us. We have all felt it. My prayer today is that we will all continue to feel His presence in new and amazing ways. At last, Megan is well. Life is uncertain, but eternity is forever.

Chapter Two **Celebrations**

Interruptions

and Signs

Life is always uncertain, but life can be pretty wonderful too. And no one loved Christmas more than Megan. It was December of 2006; she convinced me we should have a mother-daughter coffee to celebrate our favorite season. Megan quickly designed an invitation and we planned a menu. It was short notice and we thought we might have many regrets, but to our surprise sixty guests arrived at our door on December 9 to enjoy the morning. As some guests lingered and we kicked our shoes off and collapsed by the fire, Megan was elated—she had hosted a beautiful party. Mike remembered she must have said ten times, "That was so much fun!" Mothers and daughters of all ages came as we celebrated friendship and the love of the season. It would be the last time many of them would ever see their friend Megan.

The New Year

The New Year started off promisingly for Megan with a trip to New York City with college friends. Megan enjoyed her weekend, and returned home to a full schedule. In her journal, she had written out her goals for 2007. She wanted to read 30 books, take a financial management course, save for and plan a trip to Europe, all while enjoying her job as a kindergarten teacher. She had finished her master's degree the previous year and was enjoying having time to take calligraphy classes, exercise with friends, try new recipes, and enjoy her volunteer commitments at church and in the community. She loved her family and stopped by our home often. We talked on the phone every day—sometimes twice. She planned outings to flea markets, organic farms, and art shows, and was excited to have been selected to serve as a junior board member of the High Museum of Art in Atlanta. And if she was free, she would help a friend in her shop on the weekends or overnight sit for favorite families. Her calendar was full and productive.

Little Warning Signs

In February she began having some minor lapses in memory. She called me one night and said, "The weirdest thing has happened. I cannot remember how to operate the can opener." We laughed and blamed it on stress. A few days later she called sounding a little more concerned because she had forgotten the steps in wrapping a present. And one day while driving home from work she called frantically, "Mom, I cannot find the blinker. Mom, this is serious." We decided to stop talking while driving, which kept me from discovering that she was also forgetting how to use her cell phone. She made it home safely and called to let me know. Feeling totally unorganized, which was unlike her, she decided to go to her doctor. The doctor said she was experiencing stress, prescribed some medication, and told her to unschedule some things. But Megan did not get better and over the next few days she had three minor car accidents. While no one was injured, we knew there was something wrong and called a neurologist. He did an MRI, which was clear to our great relief. He also talked to Megan about stress-related possibilities. We insisted that she no longer drive, and volunteered to take her to work. Frustrated, she agreed, and we would gather enough things at her apartment so she could stay with us a few nights to make the driving more manageable.

In taking Megan to and from work, I noticed she was experiencing some difficulty with word retrieval and finishing thoughts, but she was still able to carry on conversations. She was becoming disorganized with her school work and it took her a long time to shower and dress. Her hand writing was faltering, changing from a beautiful artistic style to being almost illegible. She was so frustrated and would try over and over to write distinctly. Her hands couldn't do it and her mind recognized the difference. In late April, the neurologist asked her how she was functioning at work. She smiled and said, "Oh, I have lots of helpers. I have a wonderful aide and even though I should sign the lunch count, I let my students sign for me." When it was obvious she could not even write her own name, he put her on medical leave from work and recommended that she see a psychiatrist to help determine the source of her problems. We began to schedule appointments.

Preparation without Knowing

Thinking this was a minor issue, I continued in my job at a private school. I would call Megan, who continued to stay in our home, and check on her during the day or Mike would come home for lunch since he was close. Some days she would not answer the phone. One day when I called she answered after several rings, but was crying, saying, "Finally, I figured out how to answer." I found her one day sitting in her closet, half-dressed with her clothes on backwards. And she couldn't tell me if she had eaten during the day. As I made all these troubling observations I became more and more absent-minded at work, puzzled and worried about my daughter whose life was beginning to unravel.

It's funny how we sometimes prepare for one event and our preparation turns out to be beneficial for an entirely different one. I was in charge of a large fundraiser that was consuming most of my thoughts. It was gearing up just as Megan began to have symptoms. I was spending extra morning time in quiet study and prayer, asking God for strength and confidence to carry out my work. I was focusing on a passage in Romans which tells us to, "present ourselves as living sacrifices" in every walk of life—home, work, family, choices, dreams. As the time for the fundraiser drew near, Megan wanted to help. I guardedly assigned her to a trusted friend and she helped hand out programs, but as I watched her I knew it was not the Megan who engaged easily in conversation and confidently handled herself in social situations. She had forgotten how to shake hands and greet people. She was lacking her usual confidence. Megan was becoming very sick and I had no idea that all along, I was being prepared to venture into one of life's more difficult journeys.

In May and June, managing my job and taking Megan to her many appointments with psychiatrists, neurologists, and psychologists became difficult. I was grateful to be working in an environment that cared more about people than about fulfilling job descriptions because I certainly did not earn my pay during my final month of work. On the day our doctor called and said he had secured a bed for Megan at Piedmont Hospital, I barely remember running out of my office, not even saying good-bye to the co-workers I so loved. They bowed their heads and prayed, I know. They were my friends and loved Megan. They would become prayer warriors in the days and weeks and months ahead.

Chapter Three **Doctors**

and Hospitals

Before entering the hospital, Megan was well enough to research psychiatrists and chose Dr. Annie Cooper—she thought her name sounded British and her office was close to our home. Dr. Cooper turned out to be French and Megan loved her. We went several times a week for the intake of what would become a familiar round of questions.

Watching Megan intently during the appointments, Dr. Cooper took copious notes. Megan would try to explain, but would turn to tears of frustration and I would be called in to fill in the blanks. It was obvious Megan, with her beauty and grace, melted the heart of the professional. But the fact that Megan's abilities were silently retreating in her mind mystified Dr. Cooper and she would continue to probe with questions. When it was time to leave an appointment, Megan would ask, "Dr. Cooper, do you know what this is?" Dr. Cooper would put down her notebook, look Megan in the eye, and say with honesty, "No, Megan, I do not know, but I am going to do my best to find out." Megan, ever trusting, would smile and say, "Oh, that's great. Thank you." And we would leave with hope for a few more days.

As the sessions became more frustrating with no diagnosis coming to the surface, Dr. Cooper sent Megan for psychological testing. We went to a kind and curious doctor who completed the battery of tests over several weeks. In reading the results, I began to despair. Knowing that Megan's love of reading, learning, and conversation was quickly retreating, I had to put the report down several times before I could read the devastating findings: Megan was rapidly losing all of her cognitive ability.

By June, she had become much more disabled. Her handwriting was gone. She needed my help in daily dressing. Her walk had become an unsteady gait, and although she might sit down, she could not pull her chair into the table. In spite of troubling circumstances, Megan was able to put on a smile and her earrings (to my surprise), converse with friends a little, and be positive. It was just when we were by ourselves, she would tear up, saying, "Mom, do you know how hard this is?" and I would try my best to complete her thoughts with "to wait and wonder?" She would sometimes shake her head, and say, "I don't think...I don't think..." and would dissolve in tears. We would fall on the sofa in each other's arms and cry, and I would feebly try to reassure her with, "God knows. God cares and He is going to take care of you." When those despairing moments occurred, Megan would mysteriously and quickly drift off to sleep and wake with no recollection. I would have time to dry my eyes before her waking smile appeared.

With the psychological testing showing tremendous loss of ability, we knew the hospital was the next step. Surely something would reveal what was disabling Megan's mind. Dr. Cooper took a back seat as the doctors at Piedmont took the lead. But Dr. Cooper was there, checking on Megan, asking questions, and offering support.

As I look back, it was during this time Megan needed a psychiatrist the most. I was grateful to our first doctor for suggesting the possibility of a stress-related disorder—it opened the door to be with one trained to listen and offer encouragement. April and May of 2007 had to be the most frustrating months for Megan. Probably more tears flowed during these months of not knowing, when she was still cognizant enough to know something was seriously wrong inside her head. As a psychiatrist, Dr. Cooper gave Megan hope when hope was fleeting; she gave her empathy when there was so little to understand and much for which to be concerned. She gave her womanly support and encouragement. And she gave her a mother's compassion that lifted Megan and walked her through this hard time with the confidence that help would certainly come. I will always be grateful for Megan's choice of a special doctor.

Piedmont Hospital

On June 14, 2007, Megan was admitted to Piedmont Hospital. She had a second MRI and EEG, and for the first time a lumbar puncture (spinal tap). There was blood drawn for many types of diseases. The results of the MRI and the EEG still showed very little. The doctors looked and looked, but could not offer any definite conclusions. Nothing was giving clues to this attack on Megan's mind, but something was occurring—that was for sure.

One night at Piedmont, as Megan was drifting off to sleep, I read the Bible story of Jehoshaphat and his battle. She stopped me two or three times asking, "Mom did you call me?" I said that I had not, and continued reading although in the back of my mind I was remembering another story of Samuel and how he had been called when others had not heard it audibly. My thoughts raced back to a morning walk earlier in the year. I had some foreboding thoughts about Megan facing some trial—some inner voice warning me. I reread the passage again, asking God to help us as he had helped Jehoshaphat. I begged him. I did not want this battle and wanted God to fight it for Megan and for our family. I wanted God to "set the ambushes" and defeat whatever was attacking my daughter because she, like Jehoshaphat, "did what was right in the eyes of the Lord." I wondered if God could be calling her to some purpose—some painful purpose—and I selfishly prayed that he was not.

I prayed, writing in my journal, "Lord, may today bring a ray of hope. You said that you long to work miracles. Lord, I believe in miracles, and I ask you to heal Megan, fight this battle for her, rescue and restore her to her joy-filled life in which she loves you and serves you; if it is pleasing to you, oh God, heal her brain completely." And I asked my praying friends, who we now called Megan's Angels, to pray the same prayer with us.

After several days of inconclusive testing, Megan was to go home and rest while arrangements were made to go to Emory University Hospital for more testing. We brought her home and she fell into her own bed, smiling and relieved to be without nurses or needles. But after 24 short hours of rest, we would arrive at Emory June 18, 2007.

Emory Hospital: The Intake

There was no room on the neurology floor, so to get paperwork and procedures started they put Megan upstairs on the cancer floor. It was a corner room with a nice view. I remember the kind nurse showing me where I could get food and beverages, but I was beginning to think I would never be hungry again.

The intake nurses came to gather information and somehow humor found its way into our troubling situation. It became funny (in a sad way) that Megan could not answer the routine questions asked in a hospital, such as "Do you know your name? What day is it? Where are you?" All we could do was laugh. Megan surprised us one time, saying, "I do not know my name or why I am here." Another time when the questions began, she volunteered, "Emory Healthcare, may I help you?" There were bursts of laughter, but it was the nervous kind laced with fear.

After the initial intake, a nurse was called to draw blood. Megan was tired and the nurse could not find her veins. She called in another nurse, more skilled at finding runaway veins, but no luck for him either. Finally, they called in the cancer specialist right on our floor. Turning the lights down and closing her eyes, the doctor skillfully scanned Megan's arms, and whispered, "There it is." She explained that when a person's body is under stress, the veins recede. I think she was an angel.

The Friend

It was getting dark outside when we heard the fast footsteps of the resident doctor. A young man on his cell phone entered Megan's room, looking at his pager and rumbling through his backpack all at the same time. He looked as tired as Megan and began the familiar drill. "Do you know why you are here?" "What day is it?" When Megan could not answer any of his questions, he seemed a little impatient and walked over to her bed saying somewhat louder, "My name is Sakib, Megan. Do you know who I am?" Megan said, "Of course" and smiled at him. Sakib then prompted her, childlike, "Am I a fireman?" Megan tilted her head flirtatiously, and pointing her finger at him, shook it, and responded jokingly, "I don't think so." He blushed. She giggled. A friendship was formed.

Sakib composed himself and then turned to me and began with the list of questions, "Why are you here? When did the symptoms begin? Who has she seen? What has been done up until now? Who referred her?" I tried to answer his questions as quickly as he fired them at me, but at one point my voice broke. Pausing, I retrieved my notes and taking a courageous breath, began to read to him our journey of events that brought us to Emory. I could feel the ice melt and the young, overworked resident began to see that we were real people with real hurting hearts also seeking answers. In my mother's mind, I watched him begin to look at Megan differently, as he realized that she was his peer, highly educated like him with a bright future. The more we talked, the less he looked at his watch and at one point turned his phone and pager off and sat on the bed beside Megan. I knew it would not take long for him to fall in love with his patient.

Making the rounds with a teaching neurologist, Sakib returned the next morning with his group of classmates. I sensed in him an apology for the necessary repeating of questions. The group's entry into our room brought a hushed uneasiness as Megan, the patient, greeted all of them with her curious smile. They awkwardly circled her bed, probably stunned by the facts that were being presented: loss of memory, loss of motor skills, and loss of vocabulary. I felt the students averting my gaze and I studied each one of them as the doctor taught the lesson, which for me was all about the human connection. I learned later that several of the residents were Megan's age and I wondered what they thought, how they felt after being face to face with an unusual set of circumstances for someone their own age. I wondered if they thought about their own mortality.

The Tests

As the days passed, the tests were unrelenting. As I remember, 38 blood tests were done—that means 38 separate tubes drawn. I began to wonder if she would have any blood left in her failing body. She was becoming weaker and weaker as they did an EEG, several MRIs, and more lumbar punctures. For a child who was hardly ever at the doctor's office, she was experiencing total invasion. There were tests for lead, Lupus, and a multitude of other ailments. What could be left? I knew that the doctors were trying to find anything, testing everything to find the culprit, knowing that the frightening and fatal Creutzfeldt-Jakob disease was out there as a real possibility, but feeling that Megan's age and good health precluded it from being anything but a remote possibility. Or did it?

On Saturday afternoon we went downstairs for an MRI and I planned to return calls while I waited, but I saw another mom sitting in the waiting room, looking sad and lonely. Feeling sad and lonely myself, I turned off my phone and sat down beside her. We exchanged greetings. Her name was Pari. Her son Mohammed was ahead of Megan in the MRI line. They were the same age.

Mohammed suffered from Lupus and now had encephalitis. She was so discouraged. I told her about Megan and she began to cry. I took her hand and asked her if she would like for me to pray for our children. She nodded and we bowed our heads and prayed to the same God.

Dr. James Lah, a neurologist, came in to examine Megan. He greeted her with gentle respect and quickly became our friend. He spoke with Mike and me afterward and talked guardedly about many degenerative brain diseases. None sounded like a good option. His kindness and compassion made me crumble inside, but his professionalism made me hold myself together. He said the best scenario would be for it to be a treatable inflammation. That was the hope we needed to hear. As I shared this news with a friend, I made a statement of my faith to her. I told her that no matter what, I would hold fast to the God I loved, would not turn away, and would find strength through His love for us. But I certainly wondered what He was thinking and in the meantime we prayed for it to be a "treatable inflammation" while we waited for test results.

The Angel

Early Sunday morning, I was crying outside Megan's room when Clara, our nurse, stopped to comfort me, telling me firmly yet tenderly I had to give her to God. Later that day, when she was checking on Megan, she noticed Megan's cookbook, *Food Goes Better with Friends*. Megan had compiled it and gave copies as graduation gifts for her friends at Vanderbilt and now it seemed to give Megan pleasure to look through it. Clara asked for some of the recipes and I told her I would copy them as it would give me something to do. Sometime after midnight she returned to get them while Megan slept soundly. She was upset and crying: she had just received news that her sister had suddenly died. She came to tell us goodbye. At that moment Megan sat up and held out both arms to Clara, called her by name, and said clearly, "Clara, what can I do?" Stunned, Clara and I looked at her as if she were an angel sitting there, offering her

19

help in Clara's time of need. We gathered around the angel's bed, wrapped our arms around each other, and prayed for Clara and her family. I did not sleep that night and at one point went to a remote corner of a hallway, slid down to the floor and cried for Clara...

cried for Megan

cried for my family

cried, wondering how could I give her to God?

Going Home

On June 26, our last morning in the hospital, we woke to a blue sky striped with pink—I called it a candy cane sky and Megan nodded approvingly. I called home and Mike answered. I could tell he was crying and held the phone for him to speak to Megan. I do not know what he said to her, but she smiled and said three words confidently to him, "It is done."

I don't know how, but I tried to be upbeat for Megan as we prepared to go home. We talked—which means I talked and she followed my prompts with her eyes and smiles—about all that we had to do for the day. I read to her from her favorite devotional book, *Abiding in Christ*, and prayed for grace for the day. But I wondered silently what was happening to us.

Sakib, who by now had become a regular at Megan's bedside, came by to visit. Sakib said that Dr. Lah was working with doctors in California on some tests and would possibly have results later in the week. I wasn't sure what that meant. They wanted Megan to go home and rest. Megan raised her hand and said to her friend, smiling, "You are...you are...great!" He said "You are too!" and closed the door behind him.

I fondly remember Sakib's last visit the night we were preparing to leave Emory. A wall was covered with cards from "Megan's Angels." Flowers and gifts were overflowing our space and into the nurse's station. Mike, Owen, and Sakib sat around Megan as I began to take down the cards and sort the mementos for taking home. We talked about being hopeful, praying for a miracle, knowing that God knew everything, and trusting that He would take care of Megan and us. Oh, we sounded brave and courageous, but we were dying inside. Sakib said he admired our family's strength and attitude and was going to claim our approach as his own. He said he was just a neurologist who knew very little about so much of life. I stood there in awe, quietly realizing I had just witnessed a heart transplant on the neurology floor. In just a matter of days, a young man's heart was softened, transformed, and strengthened by a girl who did not know her own name.

Chapter Four   **The Diagnosis**
That Nobody Wanted

On June 29, 2007, we took Megan to meet with Dr. Lah at his office. He greeted us and did a few simple reflex tests with Megan and then kindly invited her to leave with an assistant so he could talk with Mike and me alone.

He described Megan as having had the "shotgun work-up" with a war-team of doctors coming at her. He spoke of brain biopsy options and what they would tell. He spoke of Creutzfeldt-Jakob disease (CJD) and abnormally folded proteins. He described brain staining and pondered how long this could have been festering. He spoke of the very disturbing age factor and that she did not fit the profile. But then he said it. "The tests are positive for CJD."

I am sure he felt as if he were speaking to mannequins from that moment on. Mike and I were frozen, unable to look at each other and staring into space as our sensitive doctor continued speaking about diffusion with weighted measuring, water movement, aphasia, and global impairment. All I could remember him saying was, "The tests are positive for CJD." He said something about medical trials in California, but all I could hear was, "The tests are positive for CJD." He said it might be helpful to get a second opinion with possibly better options for Megan, but all I could hear was, "The tests are positive for CJD."

Then he talked about the progression of Creutzfeldt-Jakob disease.
He tried to explain to us in words we would understand:

Process of degeneration – a crescendo disease

Abnormal proteins attack and multiply

Deterioration in cognitive and motor abilities

Development of Parkinson-like symptoms

Often vision problems

Possibility of jerking in the early stages of sleep

Irritability in the brain

Often die from pneumonia

All I could think about as he spoke was the horrifying information I
had read on the website describing a rare disease for which there is
no cure, and only devastating symptoms that lead to death. It could
not be true! CJD occurs in much older people. Very seldom is there
a report of someone so young being affected by this little-known
and deadly disease. Megan had been diagnosed with sporadic CJD,
meaning that the disease occurs spontaneously, and to date there is
no knowledge as to why it occurs. For some reason, normal proteins
in the brain fold over and set up a chain reaction which the body
cannot fight. Little is known as to what triggers the spontaneous
folding and within a short period of time symptoms begin to appear.
Everything that Megan had experienced was evidence of the disease
that had now been given a name.

For Dr. Lah, this must have been his worst nightmare—telling a
family their young, healthy daughter has been stricken with a rare
and fatal disease that he could not treat. With nothing to offer us but
his condolences, he must have felt so helpless. He gave us the diagnosis with every ounce of human dignity he could, looking us in the
eye, bravely saying the words that none of us, including him, could
bear to hear.

When Megan walked back into the room, I knew what had just
been said must have been a dream. She looked so beautiful and

healthy, and my heart began to fall to the floor in a million pieces. Mike and I could not even look at one another as Dr. Lah helped Megan sit down. We talked a few more minutes and then walked out, still frozen with the truth, and went to Murphy's, Megan's favorite restaurant, trying to pretend it was just another beautiful summer day. We sat at the bar helping Megan onto the stool—and ordered a Perrier. We were numb with disbelief.

I remember the waiter curiously looking at Megan out of the corner of his eye—sort of watching this beautiful young woman who needed help holding her drink. I remember hating him at that moment—I was self-conscious for her and wanted to protect her and scream at him, "She's sick! She's going to die!" I wanted to cry, but she laughed suddenly and corrected my thinking. Our lives would never be the same.

I thought of Job who wondered why he suffered so terribly. And I wondered why Megan was suffering so terribly, why so much had been taken away from her and why she was being taken away from us. No cure, no treatment plan, no options—just go home and wait in disbelief;

wait and pray for a miraculous intervention;

wait for the numbness to wear off and reality to set in;

wait for the insidious symptoms to claim this beautiful life;

wait and worry;

wait and wonder;

wait and cry;

wait and pray.

————◄►◄██

Chapter Five **Choosing to Make Sense**
When Nothing
Made Sense

$\mathcal{A}$s the news began to spread, we found
ourselves entering into a time of transitioning from the shocking
news to our response. Megan's Angels organized themselves into
a weekly prayer group and met every Tuesday at 5 p.m. They met
faithfully through the year and several times after Megan's death.
Men and women met each other for the first time, all somehow connected to their friend, Megan. A friend of mine who offered daily
support would share our prayer requests for that week and some
would pray out loud, some would pray silently, and some would cry.
Through the year, friendships were developed over bowed heads
that will be united forever in bonded hearts.

Simultaneously, a silent prayer vigil was held by a group of
golfers who met weekly at a church across town. They sat together
in silence and prayed their own heartfelt prayers for Megan and
our family. People would drive to our home and sit in their cars and
pray. Some would leave a note in our mailbox. Megan's name was
on countless prayer lists at many churches in Atlanta. Our mailbox
overflowed daily with the prayers of a community coming together
in love. Even my mailman prayed. Prayer was the one thing that we

all could do and I was so thankful for the verse in scripture that says even when we ourselves don't know how to pray, the Holy Spirit intercedes for us.[1] We were covered.

Waiting and Watching

Family and friends would come into our home to sit with Megan, hold her hand before bedtime, say the Lord's Prayer every night with us, and then go downstairs to fix our dinner while Mike and I lingered with Megan until sleep came. Sometimes, we would cry together after dinner. Sometimes, we would walk down what came to be known as Megan's Path in our garden. Sometimes, we would watch the moon come up over the trees and look at the stars. It became a sacred time of loving each other in new ways. It became a time of sensing the presence of the Holy Spirit ministering to all of us. We were all witnessing something so heart-wrenching and devastating, and yet so tender, and we were drawn to stay close in the presence of God in our hushed midst.

People would come into our home and would say they felt it—the "something" that calmed us. Yet at the same time we all felt terribly wounded. We were so hurt that God was not stepping in to restore Megan's mind even though we felt His presence among us, ministering to us, yet seemingly ignoring her. We wondered why he seemed so hidden at times—so unaware of our pleas for her healing.

Waiting and Caring

Some close friends scheduled themselves to sit with Megan for a few hours to offer their support. But what was I to do? I didn't want to go out to lunch. I didn't want to do anything. I very seldom left the house, but would instead opt to work in the garden. Why would I want to leave my child? I felt drawn to my daughter's bedside. But I soon realized that others also felt drawn. There was a peacefulness about her that compelled us to come closer. And as time went on, Megan became our child, our patient, our loved one. Everyone wanted to claim time with her. It became Megan's gift—something we all received from our patient. She drew us close, calmed our anxious hearts, made us smile, and gave us hope.

When Hospice entered our lives, they too fell in love with caring for Megan. One faithful nurse commented near Megan's last day with us, "She is my best friend and has never said one word to me." Each caregiver would lovingly tend to their tasks, making Megan and our family as comfortable as they could. It was often hard for them to leave, especially at the end. She was refreshingly young and beautiful, an unusual patient who always smiled, never complained, and melted hearts.

Mike became affectionately known as Dr. Feelgood. He maintained his composure and grieved privately and usually alone. He cared for Megan in tender ways. He would pick her up and carry her from room to room. He fixed her a waffle every morning, laughing with her over the simple pleasure of maple syrup. He brought her sunflowers—one of her favorite flowers. He watched the Food Channel and Curious George with her, often leaving for work with some profound thought to begin each day. And every night as her eyes grew heavy from the sleep-inducing medication, he would hold her hands and lead whoever was in the room in the Lord's Prayer. He gave up golf and sacrificed business for his child. His clients loved him for his devotion and came alongside him in their love and concern.

Megan's siblings, Owen and Blair, were trying to carry out their respective jobs. Owen worked for a real estate company and would often drop by for short visits—sometimes several in one day. I sensed that for Owen it was hard to bear and he needed to break up his visits. I would watch him play eye games with Megan and make faces, making them both laugh and relieving some of the anger and hurt he surely felt. Blair, on the other hand, had committed to do an internship in Florida. Thinking at first that Megan's symptoms might be treatable, we agreed. But we spent a lot of time on the telephone, assuring her and trying to help her realize that as the days rogressed, the situation was becoming more and more serious. She returned at the end of the summer and decided to stay home her fall semester of college to be close.

Waiting and Writing

While we each went about our own way of dealing with this loss, I had to figure out what I could do while I sat by Megan's side, tending to her needs and watching her every minute of every day. Because there were so many who wanted to know how best to pray for Megan, I would post updates on one of the web sites devoted to patient care. The writing was slow at first; just fragments of what we did that week and prayer requests. Megan had a large circle of friends and many were wanting to know more, to understand better, and most of all to be part of witnessing a miracle as we were all trusting that God, in His infinite power, would surely step in and change the course of a disease that I refused to even learn how to pronounce. I wrote truthfully and with conviction:

➙ JULY 12, 2007

You need to know that in spite of this vicious attack on Megan's beautiful mind, she sleeps without medication and wakes up every morning as the Megan we know and love—cheerful, upbeat, and hopeful in what the new day will bring. I for one am daily inspired by this exceptional young woman. I believe that God has already healed her and that He is using this insidious disease to show so many of us what the Spirit-filled life is all about. I am witnessing it firsthand and although it is difficult beyond description, it is a mysteriously beautiful thing.

I struggled with how to be honest about Megan's condition, yet maintain the privacy that any young woman would want—that I would want. This was not a novel with made-up descriptions of a life ripped apart. This was a life—our lives. A few days later I wrote:

➤ JULY 15, 2007

Megan has lost much of her cognitive ability. She seems to have many thoughts, but has trouble with her words, and becomes confused easily which causes frustration and tears. She listens intently, but contributes little other than a smile or laughter. She is picky about her food, but will reach for food on another's plate. She has opinions about her clothing, but cannot button a button. She faithfully puts on her watch, but cannot tell time. She insists on daily wearing her pearl earrings.

Was this helpful to know I wonder? Was I trying to explain to myself as well as others the course of a disease that was so vicious and deadly? What would I have to reveal next I wondered—and could I continue in a way that was honest and true? I wondered if I could continue to write as she slipped away, and silently held to my fervent plea for a miraculous healing.

And then, maybe because my pain was so great, maybe because my heart was so full of disbelief, I would turn to a window, away from my daughter, and find something to say about anything that would make some sense of this event in our lives. Oh, some would suggest denial. Some would ask why we weren't in a rage, screaming at God, accusing Him of not noticing us. But maybe He was noticing us.

While Megan could still put together a few words, we were trying to have a conversation about our options—which were very few. Mike said we could go underground, close our doors, and wait out the disease. Or we could choose to make the best out of a bad situation. I remember Megan becoming bright-eyed and engaged, sitting forward and struggling to get out the words "I choose...I choose" as she nodded her head positively. The decision had been made. We would choose to hold our heads up somehow and trust God for strength to face each day with hope and optimism.

And so I wrote these words a few days later.

31

JULY 17, 2007

I have learned so much about my daughter these last few months and continue to discover what a remarkable woman she has become. Her priorities, her friends, her strength of perseverance, her hopes, her dreams, her many accomplishments, her creativity, her joy of life for all around her, her true selflessness in a self-centered world, her generosity, her sense of humor, her contentment during tough times—these humble me and show me daily that I am witnessing God at work in my home, the Holy Spirit shining through her eyes and smiles most of the day, touching all of us in ways that are so hard to express—this joy in suffering. I have read about it and thought I understood it, but now I know I will never understand. It is one thing to read from scripture and try to make sense as we minister to others out of love in our Christian faith, as we quote James 1:2 which reminds us to "consider it pure joy when you are involved in various trials..." But how do we do that when our hearts are breaking—not just breaking, but screaming and yelling and writhing and hurting more than I ever thought possible? To see someone so full of love for the Lord and those around her, so enthusiastic about life in general, go through a trial such as this, makes me realize how very little I truly understand my own theology.

So I will try to put my theology in terms that I do understand—things I learn from my garden. This morning I lay in bed and mentally studied a garden path that Mike just completed along one side of our home. It is long and narrow, planted with hydrangeas, ferns, and hostas. The magnolias, camellias and crape myrtles give green walls to each side and I love to gaze from one end to the other. If I stand at one end, my eye doesn't see each and every plant, but instead my eye is drawn beyond the path—a standard rule of proper gardening I think. So my eye rests on some steps that lead me up to a distant part of the garden. The gardening work has been hard—planting, digging, watering, waiting, weeding—but as my eye is drawn through and beyond, I not only see all the beauty and work on the path, but I anticipate the beauty beyond and it pulls me through.

Because I still trust God, I know His ways are true and perfect. If we are not strengthened in our faith through Megan's illness, as painful as it is, then her suffering will all have been in vain and we will have all missed the future hope that we have in Christ Jesus. I, for one, cannot bear the thought of this trial being wasted. In my own pain right now, I am just trying to look ahead to the distant point, fixing my eyes on Jesus as I care daily for my child, knowing that God is doing something with all of this and that He has already won the victory for Megan and has a view in mind for her that will utterly amaze her with eternal pleasure. I don't know what God's view is, and right now I am fearful, so I pray for miraculous healing, knowing God is able, trusting Him with Megan, and clinging to the promise that He holds all the answers for everything.

Rereading that now, I see that the tone was set for the rest of the story. As the weeks began to run together, we approached Megan's 26th birthday and friends wanted to do something to honor her. We suggested they donate to a fund at her school as a way to express their love. Their generosity was overwhelming. I wondered why God couldn't come forth like my friends who were doing so much. I wondered where He was. Where was He as this disease advanced upon my child? Then I received a quote from a friend that said:

> "The will of God will never take you to
> where the grace of God will not protect you."

I believe that God does protect us—sometimes we just don't feel it close up. Even though I did feel God holding me together through the early part of Megan's disease, I felt that He was forgetting about Megan. Job said that he looked everywhere and could not find God, but knew that He was there and when the testing was over, he would come forth as gold.[2]

So I claimed that for Megan as the disease we feared began to march forward and manifest itself during the night in the form of hallucinations. Looking at each other, Mike and I knew full well that this was one of the first confirmations of the disease that we feared. I had never witnessed a hallucination. It was in the middle of the night and across the hall we were startled out of sleep to hear a thud and by the time we got there, Megan was jumping, screaming, and reaching for the ceiling. It took both Mike and me to get her to the bed and hold her until it completed its vicious attack. When it was over, she collapsed crying and repeating, "I am so sorry." We just held her and cried with her, knowing that it was time to call for the medication that would keep the attacks at bay.

Up to this point, we, along with Megan's doctors, had hoped that some other tests might come back and show something—anything— that could reverse the devastation. But finally, when every test was confirmed, there was nothing left but to acknowledge that Megan was going to die.

•○ AUGUST 26, 2007 *No!*

I am not sure I can see through the tears to write today, but you have been faithful in walking this journey with our family. I, too, must be faithful. I told a friend that if he was coming to see me, he should be ready to cry with me. We are not strong now, so cry with us. It will heal our breaking hearts.

This morning I searched to find the scripture that fit my weak state of mind. Psalm 34:18 says, "The Lord is close to the brokenhearted and saves those who are crushed in spirit." He promises to be our source of power, courage, and wisdom. I am clinging to this verse as I write the next paragraph. Although you have done your own research, I have been unwilling to even learn the correct pronunciation of this hideous disease.

Megan has been diagnosed with Creutzfeldt-Jakob disease (KROYTS fehlt YAH kahb), an extremely rare and fatal disease that destroys the cells of the brain in a short period of time. Symptoms of CJD may include forgetfulness, confusion, difficulty with movements, unsteady gait, muscle spasms, problems with vision, and difficulty speaking. There is currently no treatment or cure for CJD.[3]

Our friend and doctor spent two hours at our home last week, visiting with Megan, and compassionately walking Mike and me through the findings of the last MRI. He has been greatly troubled that this disease has affected someone so very young. It appears that the disease has progressed into the deeper parts of her brain. Our job is to keep her as comfortable as we can here at home with love and calm days.

And so we scream "NO!" to this vicious attack on a young person we love so much—a beautiful, kind, talented, creative, humorous, intelligent, loving, generous, compassionate, energetic woman who has had her earthly life jerked out from under her like some kind of a mean joke. We look at her physical appearance and just cannot believe what is going on inside of her. I must choose to trust that God in His mercy is shielding Megan from knowing her own limitations. She continues to bless us with her joy-filled spirit, her bright smile, her hugs, and her sociability. Last night, when Julie Andrews burst into "The Sound of Music" Megan joined in on key! And this past week, Blair and Megan have danced to Aretha Franklin. Every day when Owen walks in, there is undoubtedly recognition of her brother with outreached arms and kisses all around.

But too much of a good thing can bring her to tears, so we work hard to keep things calm with only familiar faces and limited visitation. Our dog Bodey is a faithful companion. We might not get downstairs until noon, but are thankful that we can still do the stairs.

And so yes, "The Lord is close to the brokenhearted and saves those who are crushed in spirit." He is our source which reminds us to praise and thank Him as our sustainer through this life of sorrow and joy. As my aunt wrote to Megan this week, "If God is for us, who can be against us?"

It is Sunday and Dr. Feelgood has gone to get the cinnamon sticks we all love. Megan is stirring. I will go watch her open her eyes and smile and we will love her today.

··· ◎◀▸▶━▷◈◀◈◀

Chapter Six **Finding Our Way**

The heat of the summer slowly gave
way to cooler days of vivid color. Broken and crushed, we seemed
to fall into a rhythm of daily routine—still surreal with disbelief at
the fate of our lives. Our church family and friends helped move
us through our days—scheduling visits or deliveries seemed to keep
us from turning in, closing the door on the love that was offered.
Broken and crushed makes one want to collapse in self-pity. But we
had chosen to hold our heads up and face each day with whatever
it brought. We busied ourselves scheduling visits for special friends,
making Hospice arrangements, and keeping a close eye on Megan. A
grief counselor gave good advice saying, "keep the pulse of Megan
stable and ours too as we find our way." He also made me practice
the phrase, "I know you will understand" when I felt like I just
could not talk, or come to the door, or answer the phone.

I would find myself looking through Megan's things as if I were
somehow looking for her—the Megan that was leaving us, the
Megan we missed. I ran across her cookbook filled with her lively
hand-writing and funny comments. She would write boldly YUM!
or SAVE the EGGWHITES! in the margins and place exclamation
points all over the recipe. It made us laugh and Mike said, "It's just

like her—it is the way she lives her life with an exclamation point on every day." And I realized, even in sickness, she was doing just that. She would wake every morning with a smile and laughter along with more limitations. Her joy-filled spirit was contagious in our home and began to help us in our grief along with the many followers on the website—many responded that they too were committing to live each day with an exclamation point.

The garden would beckon me outside where the floppy swallowtails were finalizing their seasonal gathering of nectar. Looking around, I discovered that the parsley was all being devoured by caterpillars. Something made me think they could be having their last meal before spinning themselves into their winter coat and hiding until spring when they would burst out with new wings to the flowering bushes, creating the show for next summer. I called my gardening friend who confirmed my thoughts. Let them feast if I want butterflies, she said. Take the good with the bad. My thoughts immediately ran to Job who questioned his friends, "Do we greedily take all the good from God and then get angry about the bad?"[4]

◆ OCTOBER 1, 2007

I have to focus intently on being grateful to God for so much good, even though many days I cannot get beyond the bad. We have Megan, sitting with us outside watching the good swallowtails and the bad caterpillars! Even though we were told she might not live but 4 to 6 months, we are crossing the 6-month mark of this journey and thank God every day for allowing her to be here in the safety of our home, for Mike's work being close and flexible, for Blair's and Owen's closeness, for my time at home, for family and friends who are walking with us. And most of all I thank God for Jesus Christ, who walks beside us daily, showing us the way to grow in character and to find purpose and meaning to life's caterpillars. God tells us in Isaiah 43:19, "See, I am doing a new thing." I know He is waiting and watching to transform.

Waiting and watching became our routine too. Megan remai
stable in her ability to walk, smile, eat, and have what we called
conversation." She could look at you intently, raise her eyebrows,
and just as quickly give you an "Oh, brother" look or a tender smile
of approval. We filled our days with reading our mail out loud, listening to music, looking at books, or visiting with friends. Waiting
with more questions than answers, we seemed to be in sort of a silent
holding pattern.

•⊷ OCTOBER 14, 2007 *Giggling with God*
A faithful card sender passed this quote along from the French mystic,
Madame Guyon, "If knowing answers to life's questions is absolutely
necessary to you, then forget the journey. You will never make it, for
this is a journey of unknowables, of unanswered questions, enigmas,
incomprehensibles, and most of all, things unfair."
I read today that if God has given you silence, praise Him for He is bring-
ing you into a mainstream of His purposes. I know that time is nothing
to God, but as we wait for answers time can really drag. Maybe the
waiting is the answer—not knowing, but trusting that somehow our
prayers have been heard for Megan's healing, and believing in our
hearts that God has a plan, and fully knowing that she is healed for
eternity by her faith in Jesus.
But where were our seemingly unanswered prayers going?
Thomas Howard says they are not lost, but hidden—"received and taken
up into the secrets of the divine mysteries, to be transformed and mul-
tiplied, like everything else we offer the Lord—loaves, fishes, bread,
wine—and then given back to us one day in the presence of the whole
host of men and angels, in a hilarity of glory as unimaginable to you
in your vigil as golden wings are to the worm in the chrysalis." [5] I love
that reference to nature, but more importantly, I do believe that the
prayers of so many are being answered in ways that truly are unimag-
inable to us in our vigil. We must trust.

I find encouragement from God's creation. If I go out early in the morning, there is Venus, winking at me in the eastern sky, saying "Here I am, steady and unchanging—all is well." And late in the afternoon when I walk to the mailbox, there is an enormous hawk, circling in front of the sunset, wings waving at me, saying, "You made it through another day—all is well."

But the best gifts come from Megan. This morning I awoke praying specifically that God would fill Megan's heart and mind with thoughts of Him, removing her from the present, giving her assurance and joy in her heart. As I tiptoed out of the room, I heard her giggling in her sleep and I gave thanks to God. There was an answer.

We wondered about so much during the fall of 2007. I suppose we expected the disease to overtake Megan faster than it did. She was content and pain free and quiet. But the nights were always a little troubling—sometimes Megan would become startled in her sleep, sit up suddenly, and look around. Sometimes she would slowly raise her arms. Remembering the ugliness of the first hallucination, we postponed using the hospital bed and opted to sleep with her so we could be close by. We would take turns, so that we each could try to get some rest in another room.

◦➝ OCTOBER 28, 2007 *Trusting with Wonder*

While I wonder about all of this in the wee hours of morning, I look out and am wowed by the full moon. I wonder about the beauty of moonlight in the quiet, how it washes blue over all I see—yet glows in a light that could never come from a street lamp. And then as the sun rises, the moon seems to compete and shines even brighter reflecting the morning rays. It appears that God has ordered another beautiful Sunday morning.

I find myself reading from 2 Corinthians 4 in Eugene Peterson's book, The Message. *The Apostle Paul speaks to me and teaches me to trust as I wonder.*

"It all started when God said, 'Light up the darkness!' and our lives
filled up with light as we saw and understood God in the face of Christ,
all bright and beautiful. If you only look at us, you might well miss the
brightness. We carry this precious message around in the unadorned
clay pots of our ordinary lives. That's to prevent anyone from con-
fusing God's incomparable power with us. As it is, there's not much
chance of that. You know for yourselves that we're not much to look
at. We've been surrounded and battered by troubles, but we're not
demoralized; we're not sure what to do, but we know that God knows
what to do; we've been spiritually terrorized, but God hasn't left our
side; we've been thrown down, but we haven't broken. What they did
to Jesus, they do to us—trial and torture, mockery and murder; what
Jesus did among them, He does in us—He lives! Our lives are at constant risk for Jesus' sake, which makes Jesus' life all the more evident in
us. While we're going through the worst, you're getting in on the best!

"Just like the psalmist who wrote, 'I believed it, so I said it,' we say
what we believe. And what we believe is that the One who raised up
the Master Jesus will just as certainly raise us up with you, alive. Every
detail works to your advantage and to God's glory: more and more
grace, more and more people, more and more praise!

"So we are not giving up. How could we? Even though on the
outside it often looks like things are falling apart on us, on the inside,
where God is making new life, not a day goes by without his unfolding
grace. These hard times are small potatoes compared to the coming
good times, the lavish celebration prepared for us. There's far more
here than meets the eye. The things we see now are here today, gone
tomorrow. But the things we cannot see now will last forever."

I was trying hard to claim the spiritual victory as Paul did, but it
just did not make sense and the pain was too debilitating. As the
days turned cooler, we held hands more often. Megan needed a
steady source of support and I learned that I could hold hands while
loading the dishwasher, checking e-mail, or putting on make-up. In

spite of her powerful grip, it offered priceless connection and much love—much like the hand-holding of those lifting us in prayer.

I began to realize how little I knew about suffering.

⊶ NOVEMBER 5, 2007

Last week, I was bold to offer the passage from the Apostle Paul. It gave me confidence and assurance reading over and over that we would not be defeated, that we could be strong in the face of sorrow, that we would not lose heart. And then I lost heart. I felt defeated and I have been gasping in a sea of tears, self-pity, and sorrow—again and again. Is there something I am not getting here?

Oswald Chambers says, "as believers in Christ, God divides our private life and makes it a highway for the world on one side and for Himself on the other. Scripture says that we are not our own, but we are to be of use to Him on our highway of life. Many will collapse in the face of heartbreak. We sit down at the door of God's purpose and enter a slow death through self-pity." Oh, I pray I do not collapse in a "slow death of self-pity."

The writer ended his thoughts by asking a hard question. "If God can accomplish His purposes in this world through a broken heart (Christ on the cross), then why not thank Him for breaking yours?" [6]

Then I remembered Philippians 4:6-7 "Do not be anxious about anything, but in everything, by prayer and petition, with thanksgiving, present your requests to the Lord, and the peace of God which transcends all understanding, will guard your hearts and minds in Christ Jesus."

I share my struggle this week because it is real and it hurts as I try to be thankful for a breaking heart. Some of you know what I am feeling— others wonder and say, "I cannot imagine." Perhaps we should try to imagine. I begin to sense this divided highway and when I ask God to hold my hand and help me to be thankful, I somehow, in my agony, sense Him guarding my heart, walking with me. Like the scripture says, it transcends all understanding. I do not understand it, but I must trust it.

Chapter Seven   **Cardinals**
Christmas and
Conversations

Megan now walked with great effort, perspiration often popping out on her forehead after doing the stairs with our help. It was like she was trying her best to make her body do what it could no longer do. She would often laugh and cry at the same time, a neurological confusion of the disease. I felt the same confusion emotionally. Blair discovered that a little chocolate could often refocus and calm these times.

It was a time when I sent very few thank-you notes for the blanket of love that covered us, all woven with the covering of fervent prayer. In gratitude I would write on the web site—feeling drawn away from my circumstances and to something that made sense to me, something that was teaching me. Megan and I would sit in the living room and look out the window. One day it came alive.

NOVEMBER 10, 2007 *The Picture That Fall Painted*
There is a canvas outside our living room window that Fall has painted. The river birch leaves are the color of mustard and closer to the window a holly is loaded with red berries. As Megan and I view our "painting," it comes to life with a bright red cardinal working among the berries in the holly tree. I wish I knew more about birds, but I do

43

know that the cardinal spends the winters here in Atlanta. Yesterday, there must have been 1,000 birds overhead, fleeing for the winter. Other birds, like robins, sort of stay around, but hide themselves. I always felt bad for the robin, remembering the child's verse, "The North Wind will blow, and we shall have snow, and what will the Robin do then—poor thing? He'll sit in the barn, to keep himself warm, and hide his head under his wing—poor thing!"

Could the winter habits of birds be teaching me something about suffering? Warren Wiersbe says that in suffering we tend to fall into three categories of coping. We can escape—flee when the cold winds come. We can endure—hide ourselves under our wings—poor things! Or we can enlist—find an evergreen loaded with nourishment to shelter us from the storm. We, unlike birds, have a choice.[7]

I will choose the cardinal this winter. Escaping is out of the question, enduring is drudgery, but enlisting is taking the winter on, finding the bright, red berries in the cold, singing when the wind blows cold, and trusting that Spring will certainly come. I am not surprised at our wonderful and amazing God—He not only gives the wintering cardinal the instinct to nest in the protected denseness of the holly, but also provides food right outside the door of his nest and places it all for us to view. How much more does he provide for us? As the song says, "His eye is on the sparrow, and I know He watches me."[8]

One particular Sunday I went to church while Mike stayed with Megan. Everything seemed so perfect at church—everyone so thankful. I returned home and walking in the door immediately thought I would be sick. How could I be thankful this year? How could we sit around the table and offer up our gratitude?

But I knew I must and I tried to make a list.

•◦ NOVEMBER 17, 2007 *Giving Thanks*

I am thankful to God for His mercy. I believe that most of Megan's cognitive ability was gone when she came home from the hospital in June. There was very little time for her to personally process her fate in this life. The Bible tells us that God does not give us any more than we can handle. I am thankful that he protected Megan from any pain and knowledge of her own condition.

I am thankful for every day—she could have been killed in one of the three accidents in March and we would have never known of the illness. It would have been a sudden, tragic loss and we would be well into the grieving process by now. As it is, we are able to hug and kiss her daily, praying that God will heal her and restore her to us. And we are able to cry and grieve with each other as we painfully watch this unfold. The Bible says to bear one another's burdens.[9] So many are bearing this burden—and somehow, I am strengthened.

I am thankful that I will never know why Megan has to die at this young age. It is not for me to know as much as I want to shake my fists at God. He does have a plan for each one of us that will one day be fully revealed. For now, it is called trust. I do know we live in a fallen world, where bad things happen to good and bad people—we are all victims of suffering. The Bible says in this world there will be suffering, but to take heart, Jesus has overcome the world.[10] Remember, in April Megan wrote in her journal as her handwriting faltered— "God, I know you have a plan and a purpose and I trust you."

I am thankful that through God's plan, Jesus has overcome this life and this world. Megan loved Jesus, and believed that Jesus conquered death on the cross and lives in Heaven, waiting for all of us to come to Him in faith and trust in a Savior who not only reigns now, but also will one day return for all of those who believe in Him and live for Him. There will be no more sadness or crying, just rejoicing. And I rejoice today that as Megan leaves this world, she confidently lives for Him.

I am thankful that as I suffer I somehow mysteriously learn more about the faithfulness of God. I have to continue to seek it out—look outside, the beauty of the changing seasons, the night sky, and the red cardinals who trust that spring will definitely come. The Bible says that because of creation, we are "without excuse."[11] It is obvious for eyes that will choose to see.

◆ NOVEMBER 28, 2007

The day after Thanksgiving, we watched the leaves come down in confetti colors. And just as quickly, there were my faithful yardmen taking them all away. For a few moments we watched them blow and flutter and pile—and then they were gone, swept away by my helpers, making the garden look orderly for a few minutes. Like the leaves still to fall, I know our emotions will continue to blow and flutter and pile up. Like the leaves, they will be lifted high in the air just to be crushed to the ground, crumbling in a heap.

And as the leaves fell, Megan seemed to lose ground. Her walk weakened, her sleep seemed restless, and her overall stamina decreased. But now, a few days later, she seems to have revived herself and the last two days have been stronger. She has laughed a lot and tried to walk alone. When she is stronger, I feel stronger, and last night I decided to pick up her journal. She was traveling from Salzburg to Interlaken on a train in June of 2003 and her words were like music.

> *"The scenery is the most beautiful. The mountains—I could look at them all day. We pass through farmland—by churches with bell towers and clouds reaching high above the little towns. The streams running alongside us are so blue. With my face pressed upon the glass I am reminded of my favorite song:*

This is my Father's world, and to my listening ears
all nature sings, and round me rings the music of the spheres.
This is my Father's world: I rest me in the thought
of rocks and trees, of skies and seas; his hand the wonders wrought.
This is my Father's world. O let me ne'er forget
that though the wrong seems oft so strong, God is the ruler yet.
This is my Father's world: why should my heart be sad?
The Lord is King; let the heavens ring! God reigns; let the earth be glad!
This is my Father's world: he shines in all that's fair;
in the rustling grass I hear him pass; he speaks to me everywhere.[12]

I am sure that so many of the people that I have encountered every day don't recognize that the world they live in—whether it is Prague, Munich, or Austria—is their Father's world. Some might not even recognize God as a significant factor in their lives. What an amazing privilege to have a God who speaks to me everywhere—through many different ways. Lord Jesus, I am so thankful for all the ways that you communicate your goodness, your faithfulness, and your love to me! Your power, your might, and your strength, too—Lord, you are so amazing!"

Even though her trip was in the summer and the leaves weren't falling, somehow it reminded me of now and I was swept away with her descriptions and love of creation as she saw many things for the first time with an understanding and appreciation for being allowed to participate fully in her Father's world. More and more, I see that she has a beautiful relationship with Jesus and I have to believe that He is speaking to her today.

I closed her journal and smiled as I went to sleep—grateful, and a little surprised that I did not feel sad, just peace in listening to her words and thinking about her many expressions of joy, awestruck at her love of the Lord.

The first of December, our friend and doctor came to visit and expressed surprise that Megan was as strong as she was, but was pragmatic in his observations and comments. We were grateful to have such a friend who loved her and wanted a miracle for Megan as much as we did.

●● DECEMBER 8, 2007 *Our Christmas Wish*

And so, Megan would be with us for Christmas, and we began to get ready. Or maybe I should say others did it for us. To our delight, our house was invaded by a team of elves who came and decorated the mantels and doors. Blair, Megan, and I sat on the sofa and watched the transformation. Another elf delivered a giant tree. Another elf put lights on the front shrubbery. And then there is the elf who gets me out of the house, the one who wraps my presents, the one who maintains my mailing list, the ones who sit with Megs, the one who drops by a fresh rotisserie chicken, the one who sends a weekly handmade card, the ones who pray. There is the team of singing golf elves and the sister elves who come to hold our hands. Love abounds.

Dr. Feelgood says that people do too much—and then he walks in yesterday with not one, but two beautiful cardinal kitchen towels. They remind me of the team that has formed around our house and I am blessed to be part of it. It takes teamwork to get Megan up and down the steps. It takes teamwork to get her showered and dressed. It takes teamwork to keep one eye on her at all times. Blair, Owen, Mike, and I are all learning more specific ways to give and take while we care for Megan.

I am waking in the night, not from worry, but from dreams and songs that I learned as a child. Thursday night I woke to these words, "Jesus doeth all things well." I wasn't sure about the song, but I knew the tune and the next morning I went to the hymnal and was able to find it. The name of the song is, "All the Way My Savior Leads Me":

> All the way my Savior leads me; What have I to ask beside?
> Can I doubt His tender mercy, who through life has been my Guide?
> Heavenly peace, divinest comfort, Here by faith in Him to dwell!
> For I know, whate're befall me, Jesus doeth all things well.[13]

I was telling my sisters who visited about the conversation in the dream. It went something like me saying, "I cannot do this. I do not want to do this." And someone else saying, "You have to do this. You can do this. Do not let temptation or self-pity get in your way. You must do this." And then I mentioned just a few words of the song and one sister said, "Oh that was Daddy's favorite hymn."

2 Corinthians 5:7 says, "we live by faith, not by sight." When we can see clearly, it is not faith, but reasoning of our mind. I have learned to rely less on reasoning and to trust my conversations in the wee hours and rely on faith to see us through.

Jesus does "doeth" all things well—he comes to us again this Christmas as Immanuel—God with us—in the middle of the night, during the day through our family and friends, and before our eyes every minute.

•➝ DECEMBER 25, 2007 *Christmas Morning*

A surprise gift arrived for Megan and was a certificate informing her that a star in the Andromeda Galaxy has been named for her! Now, we don't have a telescope, but there were so many stars out last night that I am confident I saw the "Megan Star" as I gazed at the beautiful full moon and millions of stars overhead.

A star is beautiful and mysterious—a lot like our Megan. A friend who wrote a while back described Megan's life as a polestar—that fixed position where others who have known her measure their own life by her position and confident stand. In his poetic and loving description, he also compared her life to a meteor in the night sky, where if one is fortunate to be looking at just the right time, he will be rewarded by the brilliant burst of movement—and then it is gone. But for having been watching and looking, the reward is great for getting to witness the fleeting brilliance across the sky.

This Christmas, Jesus is our bright morning star. He provides comfort and strength and, yes, joy in the midst of pain. He is the reason we have hope. He is the reason that Megan is joyful. Even though her beautiful, bright mind is fleeting, her heart is filled with worship for the one worshipped, and her joy is surprising and mysterious and real. Those who have been with her have witnessed her radiance. Mysterious—yes. Beautiful—yes. Authentic—yes.

O, come, let us all adore Him—Christ, Our Lord! He is our Joy—our Hope.

Chapter Eight **Reality Sets In**

The house became quiet in January. Blair bravely returned to college. We felt she should try to resume her life knowing any day she could be called to return home. Megan seemed to maintain some stamina, even though we watched the daily decline. Mike would sit with Megan every night as she went to sleep, but I would go outside and look up at the stars and have my cry—and my nightly say—again. I would plead with God, "Are you sure? Why can't you heal her? What are you thinking?" I would find myself bargaining with God, offering suggestions that maybe He had not thought of—such as, "Heal her now, God, and what a testimony she will have for you. She is one of your greatest fans." Somehow, looking up at the stars would silence me and remind me that all was under control, God was still in charge, Megan was in His Good Hands, and the tears would stop for the evening. My insignificance would once again take its proper place.

JANUARY 2, 2008 *Looking for the Light*
Megan woke at 3 am and I rose to give her some medicine. Sleep eluded me
    and I came downstairs to watch the sky, feeling the darkness inside
    my heart, wondering what it would be like if the sun did not come

51

up, thinking of the fear and confusion it would bring to all of us. I thanked God for a sun that always rises, for promises that will always be true, for light that always overcomes the darkness, for the first rays of morning light that assure us of an orderly creation. I know as we face the New Year it will be of utmost importance for us to look for the Morning Light, God's Light, peeking through the darkness to illumine and guide our path, however difficult our looking might be.

Megan can barely walk and we are living upstairs now. The steps have become too dangerous. She eats fairly well, but is not drinking enough liquid. Her skin is patchy. Her muscle tone is weaker, but her grip is still a grip of steel. She closes her eyes and drifts off to sleep, wakes and cries, then drifts off again. She seems to relax with medication. It seems to help her to smile and raise her eyes a little. Today we sat in the upstairs sitting room where she promptly returned to sleep and will probably sleep for several hours. It was just like yesterday, except when she awoke, she seemed surprised and thrilled, even excited at something she was seeing. She kept looking at the solid brown of the sofa, then turning to me with utter excitement, as if she had just seen the most spectacular sight and wanted to tell me. Her eyes were Megan's eyes, bright and engaged. I thought for a minute she would speak. I thought for a minute she was returning to us. This went on for about five minutes. I now call it, "the joyful hallucination." I now think she was getting a glimpse of Heaven and was seeing Paradise— her new home.

Though I do not think she will live much longer, I still believe God can heal her at any moment. I believe. I know he has a plan and a purpose and that all things work together for us who love the Lord. Megan loves the Lord, has served Him mightily, and all things are working together for God's ultimate glory.

Thinking in some way I can prepare myself, I try to envision her death. We are told she could die of pneumonia, or simply die in her sleep. She could die of starvation or die of choking. With every morsel she accepts I am fearful and thankful at the same time. I try to rehearse the end, praying that Mike, Blair, and Owen will be here. Oh, God, please! I try to rehearse the steps we have to take when she is gone:

Call Blair and Owen

 Call Church

  Call Hospice

   Call Emory

    Call Dr. Lah

     Call Family

      Call Friends

There is no reason for her to experience any pain. Comfort is possible. And somewhere in my mind I began to write her obituary.

JANUARY 14, 2008 *Living Each Day Well*

I have been reading out loud to the two of us a book called 50 Days of Heaven—Reflections That Bring Eternity to Light *by Randy Alcorn. Today I read Chapter 19, Our Old Bodies Made New. I am sure Megan did not appreciate the chapter as much as her aging mom, but I was encouraged as I read about being renewed and restored to perfect original design the way God intended for us to be. When I sit here and look at my child, I am comforted by 2 Corinthians 5:17, "Therefore, if anyone is in Christ Jesus, he is a new creation, the old has gone, the new has come." As a Christian, Megan is new with Christ in her heart and an eternal destiny in her future. She will undergo another transition at her death and resurrection. But through all the changes, Megan will still be who she was and is. There will be continuity from this life to the next. Like Job, Megan will say, "In my flesh, I will see God: I myself will see him with my own eyes—I, and not another" (Job 19:26-7). Alcorn says, " we will have the same history, appearance, memory, interests, and skills. It is the principle of redemptive continuity. God is not going to scrap his original creations and start over; instead, he will take his fallen, corrupted children and restore, refresh, and renew us to our original design." [14] And we can thank Him for what He did on the cross to make all this happen.*

So, our reading encourages us. We will not give up, but be grateful for what we have been given. We have a great future together. The gifts and talents we have tried to develop on this earth will be perfected! Megan will have her beautiful handwriting restored, and her memory refreshed, and she will be talking again with more words than she ever had! And the laugh—oh, her laugh will be exuberant! I am so excited for what God has planned for her—and each of us who trust in His promises. He does have a plan and a purpose and it is perfect.

Winter painted a new picture from our upstairs window surprising us with a blanket of snow. I remember the excitement of a "snow day" when my three children were in elementary school. We would get bundled up, make "real" hot cocoa with marshmallows, and play outside until the snow melted, which usually happened within a few hours—just long enough to make a snowman or a fort and throw some snowballs. Then the snow would vanish leaving only wet mittens, drippy boots, and happy children.

➛ JANUARY 18, 2008 *Daffodil of Hope*
Just as the snow melted, a pot of happy, yellow daffodils appeared at the door, reminding us that spring is not far away. I like knowing that the daffodil is the flower of hope for the American Cancer Society, so they have been moving with us around the upstairs to brighten our spirits. Others must be thinking similar thoughts because when I opened the mail there was a smiling daffodil card. I smile at these little coincidences, but they aren't coincidental. While Megan napped, I continued to sort her papers and found her sketch book. As I leafed through them, my eyes stopped on a page of daffodil drawings. Underneath the sketches she had written two scripture verses.
"God's holy people must be patient. They must obey God's commands and keep their faith in Jesus" (Revelation 14:12).
"Yours, O Lord is the greatness and the power and the glory and the majesty and the splendor, for everything in Heaven and on Earth is

yours. Yours, O Lord is the kingdom. You are exalted as head over
all—in your hands are strength and power to exalt and give strength
to all" (1 Chronicles 29:11-13).

What is this daffodil lesson? It's too early for them to be popping up in
the garden. Everything is waiting expectantly for winter to pass. Now
we wait. Judith Couchman in her book A Garden's Promise *says it*
well: "Spiritually, we experience barren times when it seems God has
failed us. We struggle with doubt, discouragement, broken dreams,
and unanswered prayer. We crave an expedient intervention from
God, but His schedule doesn't match ours. It feels like as though we've
been stranded in the dirt. But during these seasons we can cling to
God's promises to cultivate and spill water on our dry ground, turning
despair into hope, dust into glory. If we wait on Him during the dor-
mancy, in His time God will grant us 'a garland instead of ashes, the
oil of gladness instead of mourning, the mantle of praise instead of a
*faint spirit' (Isaiah 61:3)." *[15]

While we wait, we work at patience trying to be obedient to God through
our faith. There's another verse that says, "If you do not stand firm
in your faith, you will not stand at all" (Isaiah 7:9). And so we stand,
often with you holding us up during this difficult journey. I know the
daffodils will appear—even when winter winds still blow—and I want
to be as strong as them. I am reminded that the daffodil verses speak of
majesty and glory and splendor, everything in Heaven and on Earth is
the Lord's—even the daffodils—and yes, even Megan.

As January came to an end, the temperatures warmed a bit, giving
us a glimpse of spring. My tough, flowering quince was popping
out blooms every day in spite of the cold, assuring me it would certainly bloom even after a mean pruning a few months ago. I seemed
to watch for the strong survivors in my garden—parsley, cardinals,
and now quince.

We moved from room to room upstairs, creating a little variety
with great carry-out dinners and a variety of good music and

friends. We tried to be normal when nothing was normal. I watched Dr. Feelgood tenderly put Megan to bed, tracing his hand around her pretty face, brushing her hair back on the pillow as her eyes blinked back the sleep that the medicine encouraged. I made a mental note to nominate him for Father of the Year. I continued my routine of leaving him alone with her after dinner and I would go outside and be stricken with the beauty of the night—stars brightly shining through the barren trees. After many months of doing this, God was waiting for me and we would resume our conversation from the night before. He would begin, "Well, you made it through another day. All is well. Megan is mine." I would offer, "Please, does she have to leave us so soon? Why God? Help me to understand. What is your plan?" I am sure he tired of my repetitious questions, but still He listened and reminded me that He alone allowed Megan to stay with us almost a year with this disease—just as he allowed Lazarus a little more time on earth. We all beg for a little more time; even Jesus asked not to die. I thanked Him. My questions seem unimportant. We had been given the gift of time.

✎ JANUARY 28, 2008 *Strong to the End*

Gifts. They come in a variety of packaging—many we would never expect that surprise us with new thoughts about life. Megan's life and illness have become a gift that continues to give, teach, and unfold. This young life so beautifully lived—so sincere and private—teaches us daily. I asked Mike why God is still allowing her to be with us. It was a philosophical question to which I did not expect a response.

I opened her address book and out fell five note cards clipped together. They were colorful and in her fun style of writing. The first one said "I AM THIRD." The next one said "OBEDIENT." The third one said "ENCOURAGE." The fourth "HARD WORK" and included the scripture, "Whatever you do, work at it with all your heart as working for the Lord, not for man...it is the Lord Christ you are serving" (Colossians 3:23). And the fifth card read "CONFIDENCE" with the verse, *"Let us hold unswervingly to the hope that we profess, for He who promised, is faithful"* (Hebrews 10:23). *I turned the fifth card over and she had personalized another verse. It is from 1 Corinthians 1:4-9. Paul was affirming the faith of the Corinthians, the privilege of belonging to the Lord, and receiving His grace, the reality of their spiritual gifts. And here is her wording as she applied it to her own life—*"For in Him I have been enriched in every way—in all my speaking and in all my knowledge—I do not lack any spiritual gift as I eagerly wait for the Lord Jesus to be revealed. He will keep me strong to the end...God, who called me into fellowship with Jesus, is faithful."*

As we approach the one-year mark, I will stop asking "why" and eagerly wait on the daily revelation of the Lord.

I turned the calendar to February and was stunned by the passing days. As the daily care of Megan became harder physically, I developed a new appreciation for those in the medical profession who care for those who cannot care for themselves. I was grateful that I could be just one of the ones who provided round-the-clock care for Megan. A nurse's aide came three days a week, and the nurse came once a week. Every need was met with food and flowers and deliveries—timed, I believe, by some inner nudging. God was faithful to provide and sufficient for our needs. There was no shortage of help as many wanted to be counted in as Megan's helper.

FEBRUARY 1, 2008 *Count Me In*

This morning while having breakfast we watched Sesame Street. Mike says the more he watches it, the better he likes it. It is logical, often profound, and provides refreshing humor. I like to think it reminds Megan of her classroom. Today they sang, "Count Me In." The topic was counting, but the meaning was inclusion.

Like the Super Bowl this past weekend. From spectators to movie stars to parties in homes (even I made fresh guacamole), millions anticipate and watch the game. I am in awe of the number of fans and what they will pay for one ticket. It seems important that the beautiful people are pointed out and "counted in" at one of the biggest sporting events of the year.

I suppose life is like some big Super Bowl. We are all caught up in it, working our way to the final game, hoping to be on the winning team. God invites us to participate and provides each one of us a ticket for a future through our Savior, Jesus Christ. It is up to us to accept the ticket. And because we have been given this gift, the writer of Hebrews says we should then "run the race with perseverance to the finish." [16] It is never easy. Sometimes we get shortchanged—maybe the game doesn't go in our favor. Megan certainly did not expect to be pulled out just when life was so exciting for her. She is on the "injured list" but she chose to accept the free ticket and has played her hardest. Her name is permanently on the roster of the winning team. Even though she cannot be on the playing field of this life anymore, she is shouting mightily from the sidelines for her teammates, rooting for victory, running toward the goal. What a team player!

And she will be "counted in" at the victory celebration in Heaven. We are all invited.

It was Valentines Day and I dressed Megan in pink pajamas with hearts on them. Regardless of her losing ground, we were sure of our love for her and each other. Mike and I watched her doze and reminded ourselves of our love for each other, Megan, Owen, and Blair, and our family and friends. We did a quick inventory of our blessings and thanked God for the abundance of love in our lives.

⊸ FEBRUARY 14, 2008 *Feeling God's Love*

Love. The Beatles sing the song, "All You Need is Love." The Bible says "God is love." Does that mean all we need is God? This morning I was mindlessly looking at the things on my desk. One is a silver cross I use as a paperweight. It has LOVE etched across the top. Another is a little heart magnet stuck to my lamp that says "Love Never Fails." If God is love, then does that mean God never fails? I am counting on it.

It is when we choose our own way and not God's that causes us to fail, to lose our direction, lose hope, lose out on true love. Mark 12:29-31 very simply states to "Love God. Love others." The first part instructs us to love God with all of our hearts and souls and minds. We have to do that before we can love others, which is the second part. In learning more about Megan, I have discovered just how very much she loved God and felt so loved by Him. Because she felt God's love, it was natural for her then to love us and those around her in such generous fashion. That has been returned to her in countless ways this year. She has experienced true love.

I read that we all like to listen to the personal testimony of others, but we don't want God himself to speak to us personally for fear of having to do something we don't want to do. With that attitude, we deny God access to our lives. If God is the source of all love, then it would seem that whatever He asks us to do won't fail us in the long run. And because He loves us, He does want us to love Him back. It is a relationship.

He wants to be our first love. When we acknowledge God—the source of true love in the world—as central to our lives (instead of ourselves), we feel so loved and cared for that we can easily reach out to a hurting world and love those around us. Jesus gave us that example. And Megan has been and is in that kind of love—forever.

Just before getting sick, Megan wrote in her journal,

> *"Oh Lord, to have the confidence to be able to serve and love you with no hesitation and few worries—oh, I long for that! Oh, Lord, I pray at this very moment that you would be growing me into who you would have me to be—at this very moment you would prepare me for that and I would be amazed at your perfect plan for my life—and thankful. God, I so wish I knew how you worked but since I don't, help me to love and trust you like never before. Thank you for the blessings in my life—help me to see them as blessings."*

✦ FEBRUARY 22, 2008 *No Hesitation and Few Worries*

And then Megan's forgetfulness began to increase. Her frustrations increased with her own inability to function at her normal speed. As a teacher, she kept her sense of humor and allowed her kindergartners to write for her as she realized some days she could not form the letters. She said, "You should see their eyes light up when they realize they are writers!" She took it upon herself to get to her doctor and have a check-up. Normal and healthy, just stressed, said the doctor. So she ratcheted back her schedule. But the symptoms increased and she became more and more frustrated, but still trusting and thankful. Being young and healthy kept us all from being overly concerned. Looking back one year, I now see that her positive spirit and seemingly good physical health were disguised blessings that probably masked the invisible culprit of deadly activity building momentum, hidden in her bright and beautiful mind, starting it's march to destruction. It was a blessing that kept her spirits up as she tried to get well. Her journaling gave her strength. She talked to the Lord throughout— while she could write—trusting and loving the One who cared for her. She was in fact as I look back "able to serve and love God with no hesitation and few worries" as her journal read.

I have said before I believe that God protected Megan from knowing that her life was about to take a major turn—a turn that would alter her plans for 2007 and beyond. I consider that a miracle and a major blessing. Every doctor gave her hope through the progression of stages. Each one fell in love with the joy and enthusiasm she was able to bring to every appointment, always smiling, trusting, and thanking them for their help, always hoping they would find the answer to her mysterious troubles.

And they did...and here we are...one year later trying to be brave like Megan, trying to trust and "serve and love with no hesitation and few worries." God in His mercy protected Megan from the pain of knowing her disease or its prognosis. He has allowed us that knowledge and watches to see what we do with it. In our shock and hurt, we do not suffer alone. That is what the cross of Christ teaches us—and I am learning as I go.

Henri Nouwen wrote, "We will suffer, and suffer with one another, but in doing so we will uncover nothing less than the presence of a God whose consolation keeps us going." He goes on to say "Pain suffered alone feels very different from pain suffered alongside another. Even when the pain stays, we know how great the difference if another draws close, if another shares with us in it. This kind of comfort comes most fully and powerfully visible in the Incarnation, wherein God comes into our midst—into our lives—to remind us that He is always with us. In Christ, God draws near us amid our sufferings. There is no human suffering that has not in some way been part of God's experience. That is the great and wonderful mystery of God becoming flesh to live among us. God becomes a part of our mourning and invites us to learn to dance—not alone, but with others, sharing in God's own compassion, as we both give it and receive it." [17]

Chapter Nine **Do You Love Me?**

Blue skys, daffodils and blooming Lenten Roses gave the definite promise of an early spring. We opened the upstairs windows and enjoyed fresh air and our cardinals calling "Whata-cheer-cheer-cheer!" Megan slept most of the time, but could wake up enough to eat some lunch or down a milkshake brought by a friend. I bought a new food processor to make eating easier so she could eat whatever we ate, just pureed. I could not bear for her to stop eating and she didn't seem to mind if the Chicken Divan looked like guacamole.

And when I wasn't cooking, I read. I read in John 21 where Jesus appeared to his disciples after his resurrection. After cooking for them, he turned to a more serious discussion and pointedly asked Peter three times if he loved him. Peter was at first a little annoyed Jesus kept asking him, but the third time said, "Lord you know everything, you know I love you." Jesus told him to pour himself out for others—to feed sheep. When Peter questioned Jesus about his peers, Jesus simply told Peter to follow Him and not be concerned about the others. It seemed to be a lesson for me, asking me over and over if I loved the God who was not answering my pleas. It made me squirm inside to think He was instructing me to pour myself out when my pain was so great. Follow Jesus. Feed sheep. And on those times when I could muster the strength to help someone else, I would be filled with a strength that was enough for that day.

And then I read about the simple, profound writings of the French monk who cooked in the monastery in the 1600's. In his book *Practicing the Presence of God,* Brother Lawrence said, "the heart must be empty of all things, because God will possess the heart alone, and as he cannot possess it alone without emptying it of all besides, so neither can he act there, and do in it what pleases, unless it be left vacant to him. To live in the presence of God is to live with purity of heart, with simplemindedness, and with total acceptance of his will. That demands a decision and great courage." [18]

━● MARCH 5, 2008

I am trying to muster this kind of courage in giving the Megan who still fills my heart completely to God, allowing Him to fill my heart, trusting that He will fill the loss of a daughter and friend who is coming to Him. Total acceptance of God's will is hard. Simplemindedness is hard. Purity of heart is hard. We think we can do it until we are asked to do something that makes our hearts turn and run. But gradually giving God more and more space seems to dull the pain somewhat and replace it with some new kind of possession that guides our hearts and lives in a direction different from our desires.

I find myself becoming quieter, more removed, more in solitude. Dr. Feelgood calls it "going underground." Whatever we call it, we are not idle, but busy seeking God's face, sitting before Him, giving him our hearts, handing him Megan over and over again, reaching out to others who are hurting in their own journey of suffering. Jesus, our Shepherd, said very simply to feed His sheep and like Peter, I have to be asked over and over if I love Him.

Jesus said in Mark 12:30 that the first commandment is to "Love the Lord your God with all your heart and soul and with all your mind and strength." I suppose when those four come together we will have peace—God's way.

Our doctor came from Emory and spent time with us. He said the hard things gently, lovingly. He said he will never have another patient like Megan—she is a lonely statistic–one in 100 million. One day I hope to be able to understand this Creutzfeldt-Jakob disease, but as Dr. Lah says, it is so rare and so little is known, there is not much available to know. He asked if Emory could have her spinal column as well as her brain for research. We said of course. Megan, the giver, had given so much to so many.

MARCH 17, 2008 *The Giver*

Two letters came for Megan in the mail and both remind me of Megan, the giver, before illness struck. One was an invitation to celebrate the release of a new cookbook. Oh how she loved to cook for others! The other was an invitation to a volunteer meeting. Oh how she loved to volunteer! This year she has given us her smiles, laughter, and hugs; she has given her friends the opportunity to be with her; she has given— or will give—her organs to medical research; and she has given people she doesn't even know hope and courage to face the unthinkable.

I am grateful for all that she has given, especially her gift of journaling since 1995, writing her thoughts to the Lord, giving Him her devotion and love. Now I look at her and I think about all the things she loved to give and now cannot. Her abilities to write and create are gone. She cannot think. Even her smiles are fading. But she gave her heart to the Lord and it is beating regularly with Christ's love. That love will never let her go. She is giving up everything in this life, but God, the giver, is holding her and caring for her and giving her a new life as her old life fades.

So here we are during Holy Week of Lent thanking God for what He gave to each of us—the gift of a new life with Him—free to all who will accept it. I am reminded by scripture to be thankful. Romans 8:31-34 says, "What, then, shall we say in response to this? If God is for us, who can be against us? He who did not spare his own Son, but gave him up for us all—how will he not also, along with him, graciously give us all things? Who will bring any charge against those whom God has chosen? It is God who justifies. Who is he that condemns? Christ Jesus, who died—more than that, who was raised to life—is at the right hand of God and is also interceding for us."

It was Easter Sunday and Mike and I were able attend worship while Owen and Blair sat with their sister. We listened to the message of the resurrection. I felt as if we were practicing for Megan's service—seeing our pastors and friends, singing songs of rejoicing, and praying prayers of victory over death. We intended for her service to be just the same—rejoicing that God had freed her from disease, and made her perfect in His eyes. We planned to celebrate her resurrection.

MARCH 23, 2008 *Show Us the Way*

I am troubled that I was asked why I did not address Megan's physical condition more in my writing—give more details and post current pictures of Megan. My best answer is that the most important thing is to care for Megan with dignity and grace, to treat the beautiful 26-year-old in the manner in which she was used to living. The ugliness of any disease is best learned through research on one's own—the reality is enough for the eyes of those who love her the most. Why should I subject her to humiliation, and distract others from the real message of this journey?

Today, as I end my Lenten devotional book, Show Me the Way *by Henri Nouwen, I am reminded of Megan's condition. He writes of a disabled young man destined to a new life, a resurrected life. "In his new body he will carry the signs of his suffering, just as Jesus carried the wounds of the crucifixion into his glory. And yet, he will no longer be suffering, but will join the saints around the altar of the lamb. It is a great and powerful mystery. What a faith! What a hope! What a love! The body is not a prison to escape from, but a temple in which God already dwells, and in which God's glory will be fully manifested on the day of resurrection."* [19]

With Megan still with us, I am strengthened by this hope and promise of Easter. It is good timing for which I am thankful. God is dwelling in Megan. With every day I feel His presence more and trust her completely to His care. She is His.

Last week, Dr. Feelgood shared a quote from one of his favorite books. In The Grapes of Wrath, *John Steinbeck is describing the move to California from Oklahoma. The Okies are sorting through their belongings and are forced to leave much of their lives behind. The question is asked, "How will we know it is us without our past?"* [20] *And so we have been asking ourselves the same question, "How will we know it is us without our Megan?" It is one we think about constantly and wonder as we grieve her leaving us. But I must go back to her words in her journal—her last entry that reads, "God, you have a plan and a purpose and I know it is good and I trust you." Somehow, we will find our way.*

Oh, God, show us the way.

Our emotions were like the uncertainty of riding on a rolling, curving bike path: what would be over the next rise or around the next bend? We accepted more and more the reality of her impending death. We were held by love that carried us a little further down this road. The days flew. Nights brought rest. I would walk outside and the beauty of creation would take my breath away. The God who opened the apple blossoms outside our door was the one who was holding our hands. The God who brought a cardinal to me every day was the one who whispered, "I am with you. All is well. Stick with me." I had few words—possibly from the fear of not being able to stay the course. I was told that the prayers of our friends were becoming silent as well, waiting and listening for God.

●◦ APRIL 7, 2008 *A Powerful Presence*
In my heart, there is joy right there along with the pain. Owen had dinner with us last night and Blair called from school early this morning. I

remind them how much they are loved even though it seems so much attention is now focused on Megan's needs. We are all trying to learn to think less of ourselves and more of others.

And you continue to care for us in ways that would seem mysterious. How does the one who brings fresh-picked strawberries know that home-made custards were just delivered? How does the birdwatcher know when the feeder is empty? How does my high school girlfriend know I have wanted the book about hymns and their origin? How do the waking moments before dawn bring words and music to my mind and heart of those hymns that I grew up learning at the little church in Kentucky? How is one prompted to call or just sit on my street and pray for this child and our family? How?

Some might say, oh, it is just coincidence. Or, people are just morally conscious of doing the "right" thing when a tragedy strikes. Maybe both are somewhat true, but there is something more that touches our hearts. Jesus told the disciples that He would be sending them the Holy Spirit to be with them and to guide them in all things and, prompt them to action. And he did. As believers in Christ, we have the same Holy Spirit working in and through us. As my visiting nurse quietly said today, "The Holy Spirit doesn't need us to beg Him to come down. He is everywhere, gently and lovingly available to those who believe."

Owsald Chambers says that the term "Holy Spirit" is actually another name for the experience of eternal life working in human beings here and now.[21] Eternal life working here and now—I had to repeat that to myself. It is why I can feel joy when it doesn't seem reasonable. It is why someone who loves the Lord is prompted to reach out a hand. It is why I can cry and trust God at the same time now. It is why I can look at Megan and witness eternity here and now. It is why I some days feel like I am being carried by some unseen and powerful force. But I have to be the one who allows it to come in and to work in me and through me. I have to denounce fear, worry, and selfish desires. I have to decide to welcome a presence that I cannot see or touch, but that guides my heart to truth and brings a sense of joy and peace. It is my daily work. Galatians 5:22 promises, "But the fruit of the Spirit is love, joy, peace, patience, kindness, goodness, faithfulness, gentleness, and self-control."

Megan waited quietly. Nothing much was on her mind. She did not have her organized, red day timer opened to April 25th. She was not planning her weekend. As I sat beside her and looked at her patient calmness, I chose to believe that even though her mind was separated from friends, duties, cares of this world (and yes, even me), her spirit was connected with Jesus and her joy came forth in wonderful, surprising ways. She would return a smile and laugh her perfect laugh. She would pat our hand. She would raise her left hand in a mysterious expression of praise.

➻ APRIL 25, 2008 *Waiting*

I read about "quietly" waiting on the Lord and a verse greets me every morning and reminds me, "...in quietness and trust is your strength..." (Isaiah 30:15). I read that if we are to have our whole heart turned toward God we must have it turned away from ourselves, from all that occupies and interests us, good and bad. So I have to believe that Megan's whole heart is now turned to God. And I praise Him that He is still with her now that her earthly cares are gone. Of course, Megan did not make that choice willingly—to succumb to a dreadful disease, but she did decide long ago when life seemed easy and there was much to accomplish that God would reign in her heart. It is still her best decision. A high school friend wrote to Megan and simply stated "Megan, at the end of the day, all any of us have is God." How true and profound as we wait with her.

I stumble over the fact that God wants our whole heart and yet we have to get to a tight place, even death, to finally give up and give him all of ourselves. What a mystery it is that we fight for this life to be full and productive of many things that might or might not be so godly, and yet to know at the end of the day—when we crawl into bed—all any of us have is God.

Maybe I am learning to wait because I have been so removed from day-to-day life this year. I watch Dr. Feelgood come and go. I watch Owen and Blair come and go. I listen to my friends talk about their activities. They downplay them thinking how left out I must feel. But I do not feel left out—in fact, I feel more included than I ever have in a profound journey of my own heart. Maybe it is through the quiet waiting God has pulled me aside and gotten my attention in new ways.

The spring mornings were beautiful and Megan's smile was all we needed to give us energy for the day. Outside, the May garden was becoming a celebration of blooms—roses, irises, dianthus, and peonies. The day was Cinco de Mayo and Dr. Feelgood and I decided to celebrate Mexico's victory over the French with chicken enchiladas with extra cilantro and lime. We looked for little things to celebrate. Dr. Feelgood could always find something. When Megan was in the hospital, the nurses said our room looked like a French café when he would bring candles, flowers, and carryout from her favorite restaurants. Who wanted hospital food when you could have a crab cake from Murphy's?

◦➌ MAY 5, 2008 *Celebration and Sorrow*

We celebrated at the wedding of a good friend. It was a gift to be a guest and part of such a joy-filled occasion. I teared up only out of love for my friend who was a beautiful, radiant bride. Tears can flow when celebrating just as easily as they can when in sorrow. I read somewhere that they are the heart's deepest expression when there are no words. I seem to be losing my vocabulary.

If we look closely, we all find ourselves somewhere between celebration and sorrow, light and dark, life and death. The big moments of life—birth, death, marriage, anniversaries, achievements, tragedies—all

seem to mark the years, but the day-to-day is where our obedience
steps in and decides if we will face the day with celebration or sorrow.
In this, our darkest hour, we seem to be celebrating in ways that carry us
through our sorrow. Oh, not in fireworks and fanfare, but just in the
simple everyday events showered with love and tears. Family life is
strong, friendships have never been deeper, and God is with us. Mostly
He seems silent, but as He watches over and cares for Megan we feel
His presence while we wait upon Him.
The good news is that sorrow for the believer in Christ always ends in celebration. Death does not have a victory. God's ability to restore life is
beyond understanding. I just have to trust it and wait for it. I have
to trust that God is restoring Megan for His purposes and one day I
will say, "Oh, so that is why you needed her at the age of 26." But I
confess I continue to remind God that I think it would help just to have
a glimmer of His plans now—just a peek. But like the old song says,
"Farther along, we'll know all about it, Farther along, we'll understand why; cheer up my brother, walk in the sunlight, we'll understand
it—by and by." [22]

MAY 13, 2008 *Discouragement*

Discouragement is not having courage to move forward. Maybe it is being
tired of waiting on a situation that does not improve and feeling helpless to do anything to change it. Discouragement is not quite knowing
how to continue to be strong when I can feel so weak at watching the
oh-so-slow deterioration of my child—discouraged at feeling alone
and lost in spite of the many faithful friends who give without expecting anything in return. Just a few minutes ago a warm coffee cake was
delivered to our door. Today I do not feel worthy to receive such love
because of this "stew" of human emotion. What has happened to my
courage and faith?
But here are two of those coincidences that nudge me back to truth and
offer help to climb out of my "stew." Yesterday the mailman delivered
a little book, Abiding in Christ, by Cynthia Heald. Today I opened to

May 13 and the title is "Protection from Discouragement" with the scripture from Deuteronomy 31:8 that says, "The Lord himself goes before you and will be with you; He will never leave you nor forsake you. Do not be afraid; do not be discouraged."

And here is the other coincidence. At my desk this morning, I turned to one of Megan's journals. Out came a piece of paper. At the top she had written, "Abiding Verses to Memorize" From the same book that arrived yesterday, she had written three verses for her reflection and study (with some personal notes). These notes were now encouraging me.

Abiding in the word

"I have not departed from the command of His lips; I have treasured the words of His mouth more than my necessary food" (Job 23:12).

(How easy is it for me to depart from the Word and busy myself with busyness?)

Choosing to abide

"She had a sister called Mary, who sat at the Lord's feet listening to what he said. But Martha was distracted by all the preparations that had to be made. She came to him and asked, "Lord, don't you care that my sister has left me to do the work by myself? Tell her to help me!" (Luke 10:39-40).

(I am a master of distraction.)

Security of abiding

"Remain in me, and I will remain in you. No branch can bear fruit by itself; it must remain in the vine. Neither can you bear fruit unless you remain in me" (John 15:4).

(It is hard to grow when I am concentrating on my own discouragement.)

I will consider this her Mother's Day card for 2008.

•○ JUNE 17, 2008 *In Appreciation of Dr. Feelgood*

Last June, Megan and I made a card. She picked a sunny, yellow marker and scribbled a round shape. I added sun rays and taking her hand in mine, we wrote, "Happy Father's Day." We gave it to Mike when he arrived at the hospital. She was more creative the summer of 2002 when she studied at Focus on the Family Institute in Colorado. She made three signs. One said "Happy," one "Father's," and one "Day." She went to three scenic places and had a friend take her picture in front of The Garden of the Gods, Pike's Peak, and one in front of the institute's sign. She put them all together and created her own personal greeting for her dad. Megan showed her appreciation for those she loved. And in her most creative way to date, she is still giving her love through God's spirit that resides in her.

We don't always think to show our appreciation for the people around us who inspire us, who challenge us to be a little better, especially when life is "good." And then they leave us and we discover what we loved about them. I am thinking of the popular newsman Tim Russert who passed away this weekend. Like so many others, I liked him—smart, considerate, with a generosity of spirit that always stood out. His colleagues said he would always remind them to do three things: be prepared, be polite, and be ready with the tough questions. A good way to live, I think.

So, I know my children will join me in saying today how much we appreciate our own Dr. Feelgood. Like the one in the news, he is smart, considerate, and has a generosity of spirit that carries us on many days that have been "not good." Someone has said that character is what you do when no one is watching. And "still trying to be invisible" Mike has put work in perspective to help at home, declined golf for a season, and has taken an active role in Megan's daily care—he stands out and I am inspired by my husband and friend.

We work to maintain the qualities Russert insisted upon and there is much in scripture to back up each of them.

We try to be prepared.

As hard as it is to do, we try to maintain a routine when nothing is normal. We have struggled doing the difficult jobs of preparing for Megan's service, making arrangements for assisting with research, and, of course, accepting our loss.

"I can do all things through Christ who gives me strength" (Philippians 4:10).

We try to be polite.

You would think politeness comes naturally, but sometimes under emotional strain an occasional irritability will flare—forgiveness is a wonderful thing.

"The Lord is gracious and compassionate; slow to anger and rich in love" (Psalm 145:8).

We face the hard questions.

Will we work through our grief in a healthy way? Can we find meaning when life doesn't make sense?

"Let us run with perseverance the race marked out for us. Let us fix our eyes on Jesus the author and perfecter of our faith, who for the joy set before him endured the cross, scorning its shame, and sat down at the right hand of the throne of God. Consider him who endured such opposition from sinful men, so that you will not grow weary and lose heart" (Hebrews 12:1-3).

Chapter Ten The Source of Her Joy

Drifting into the arms of God seemed to gently express Megan's activity. We had to look harder to see that she was still breathing and would breathe a sigh of relief when we touched her and she was warm. Eating had now become her only activity and I worked hard to give her nutritious and creative foods: cheese omelets cooked in not one, but two tablespoons of butter; peanut butter banana yogurt smoothies; new potatoes and parsley pureed with grilled salmon; fresh-picked strawberries blended into a vanilla milkshake, and of course Dr. Feelgood's daily, waffle smothered in butter and maple syrup. It was the one thing she would chew enthusiastically. We scheduled massages for Megan's arms, legs, and shoulders. I read to her and did needlepoint. I could make it sound like we were on a cruise ship.

MAY 21, 2008 *Discovering Our Heart*

The darkness of discouragement has lifted. I have seen God reveal himself in ways that only He is able to do, mostly because He is God and always is revealing His nature, and somewhat because others were praying and angels were flying our way. I say it in that order because God is becoming so much bigger and stronger to me these days—maybe because I am seeking His face more, watching for Him, focusing on

His majesty and wonder, understanding more that the longings I experience in my heart all begin and end with God.

A book that Megan refers to in her journal called The Sacred Romance *has pulled me in. I am only a third into it, but am drawn to read instead of write or even cook, as I rediscover a story that was written so long ago. It is a story about our heart and the discovery and loss of it—the mystery and source of its longings. It is as simple as looking at a sunset, or as complicated as telling one you love good-bye. It is when we tear up at the joy of an experience together that goes beyond just the experience itself, like the birth of a baby or a wedding. It is that ah-ha moment when we finally feel connected, but sometimes not sure of what has made the connection. The author Brent Curtis says, "In the end, it doesn't matter how well we have performed or what we have accomplished—a life without heart is not worth living. For out of this wellspring of our soul flow all true caring and all meaningful work, all real worship, and all sacrifice. Our faith, hope, and love issue from this fount, as well. Because it is in our heart that we first hear the voice of God and it is in the heart that we come to know him and learn to live in His love." [23]*

I am reminded of one of Megan's favorite hymns, "Come Thou Fount of Every Blessing." Fount is defined as "source." God, the source of every blessing, is offering us life to the fullest and as the last lines say, "Prone to wander, Lord I feel it, prone to leave the God I love; Here's my heart, Oh take and seal it, seal it for thy courts above." [24]

I read that while we wait, God waits also on us, preparing, leading, and helping us through this long, dark valley. I could feel it in my heart and knew that as this dark valley persisted, solitude became more and more of a way to totally allow God full control of my pain. But on those occasions when we needed to put ourselves aside and be with others in their celebrations, we could still amazingly find joy.

➣ MAY 28, 2008 *Bach's Intent*

As we sat in the sanctuary waiting for the bride, I could feel the welling
of unwanted tears and knew I could not—I would not—let myself
fall apart at this happy occasion. It would have been okay though.
Everyone knew our situation and we all were trying to be present at
the wedding and not in our grief over Megan. The music played the
familiar "Jesu, Joy of Man's Desiring," one of Bach's little choruses.
I did not know the words, except for the title, so in contemplative mode
I repeated to myself, "Jesus, Joy of Man's Desiring, Jesus, Joy of my
desiring, Jesus, you are the joy of all that I desire, Jesus, Jesus, Joy,
Joy." I made it through with joy, and maybe one tear.
I have been humming the song ever since. I read that Bach never intended
it to be performed quite so slowly, but lively and with great joy. I loved
that I found such meaning in the words.

> Jesu, Joy of Man's Desiring,
>   (original translation: Jesus shall remain my gladness)
> Holy wisdom, love most bright;
> Drawn by Thee, our souls aspiring
> Soar to uncreated light.
> Word of God, our flesh that fashioned,
> With the fire of life impassioned,
> Striving still to truth unknown,
> Soaring, dying round Thy throne.
> Through the way where hope is guiding,
> Hark! What peaceful music rings;
> Where the flock, in Thee confiding,
> Drink of joy from deathless springs.
> Theirs is beauty's fairest pleasure;
> Theirs is wisdom's holiest treasure.
> Thou dost ever lead Thine own
> In the love of joys unknown.[25]

Certainly, the words are fitting for a wedding, but I believe Bach's intentions were on a higher plane—one that expressed a relationship with God and his world. The Bible speaks in Matthew of Jesus as the Bridegroom and His coming for His bride, the body of believers.[26] *In Ephesians Paul teaches about marriage being modeled after Christ who loved the world.*[27] *How like God to create marriage as an example of His love for us. As the book I am reading says, it is a "sacred romance."*

Megan, too, will be a bride—the date has been set, but no "save the date" cards will be mailed. Jesus will come for her "through the way where hope is guiding...in the love of joys unknown."

The sun rose early. After making coffee, I would roam around the garden for a morning cry. The bright "Heavenly Blue" morning glories greeted me as I paused to study their exquisite color and design. Striking in beauty, but fragile and short-lived, I admired the blooms before their evening departure. Nothing lasts forever.

I would return upstairs to watch the same death process overtake Megan and I began to let go of her as the ugliness of it advanced. As Megan lost weight, her features became unfamiliar. Her once beautiful skin began to break down in places and I hated myself for not being strong enough to tend to her final physical needs. But Hospice was there, taking over what I could no longer face. I felt so guilty and helpless. And then I wanted it to be over. I hated death and what it had done to life. I found myself cheering silently for Megan to take her last breath and run into the arms of Jesus. There, she would be free.

JUNE 24, 2008 *Love From the Heart*

Everything dies. Henri Nouwen says that death must become part of our present. "As we break through our need to cling to what we have, what we know, what we possess, we can be liberated by trustful surrender to God. Then our anxiety will not cripple us, but point us forward in joy, point us even to what we cannot predict or fully see, even our own death. Indeed, the New Testament paints a portrait of an eternal life that begins now: 'See what love the Father has given us, that we should be called children of God; and that is what we are...Beloved, we are God's children now; what we will be has not yet been revealed. What we do know is this: when he is revealed, we will be like him, for we will see him as he is' (1 John 3:1-2)." [28]

I still feel disappointed when the morning blooms are gone so quickly, even though I know fully that this is the way of life. Nouwen goes on to remind us that even Jesus cried out, "My God, My God, why have you forsaken me?" He quoted the words of the Psalmist, who for all his sense of forsaken abandonment, still called upon God. "Absence and presence touch one another. The God the psalmist fears has turned his gaze away, but is still a God the psalmist can address. The One who seems far from our plea is the One to whom we still turn."

I reassure myself that He is in charge of Megan even though He seems to have turned away. He loves her more than we do and is planning her day of entrance into Heaven. A friend wrote last week and mentioned the word "love." It seems to connect everything we do—especially in death. She said, "I don't know what she experiences, what she understands, if anything, but I am sure that even though higher thought functions have disappeared, she can still feel the attention, and the presence of your love." And the love that we offer is the love we have been shown from our Father in Heaven. Once we have that kind of love, it never lets us go.

Today, Megan's caregiver said, "I love Megan. She has become my best friend even though she has never said one word to me." Her statement struck me and I know this to be true and have watched it happen. The only explanation for me comes from John 7:38 that says, "Whoever believes in me, as the scripture has said, streams of living water will flow from within him."

I told Megan this afternoon that I was so very proud of her for refreshing so many. God is using her mightily.

We had passed the one year mark since Mike and I sat in our doctor's office and received the fatal diagnosis for Megan. At that time we thought we would be lucky to have her with us six months. We were all stunned at her stamina and that she could still radiate joy. But her brown eyes often seemed to be looking at something beyond our walls. She was slipping away in the same manner in which she lived her life—quietly, confidently, and oh, so gently. I felt she had some message for all of us in the way she would look at the wall above her bed that by now was covered in crosses and scripture plaques that had been sent through the year. One little cross with "joy" written on it was just in her reach and she would often touch it. Many times it would be next to her in the bed. It was like she was leading us.

➤ JUNE 29, 2008 *Looking Beyond the Walls*
Much of my thinking is done when I walk with Bodey, our black lab. Today it turned into a power walk with God. Even though it was short, I came home fresh and strong, feeling like I needed to say a few specific things to honor God before my weekly writing comes to an end. You see, a friend reminded me that she is always hearing of new people reading about Megan and following the story. What started as a convenient way to tell family and friends about Megan has turned into something that seems to have a life of its own. I said, "But there is not much new news about Megan and what I write about is not a new story. It is an old, familiar story of pain and suffering with a theme weaving through our lives in miraculous ways, always return- ing to the Cross of Christ." And as so many wait and watch for Megan to leave this life, I think she would want all who are waiting with her to know in their own heart and mind that they too have received the gift of salvation and have a place in Heaven reserved with their name on it, alongside Megan. It is sometimes called "the invitation."
I remember learning about the Four Spiritual Laws growing up. "Just as there are physical laws that govern the world, there are spiritual laws that govern our relationship with God." [29] *I am confident Megan understood and abided by these principles.*

LAW I GOD LOVES US AND OFFERS A WONDERFUL PLAN FOR OUR LIFE (*John 3:16, John 10:10*).

LAW II MAN IS SINFUL AND SEPARATE EVEN THOUGH WE WERE ORIGINALLY CREATED TO BE IN A LOVING RELATIONSHIP WITH GOD (*Romans 3:23, Romans 6:23*).

LAW III JESUS CHRIST IS GOD'S PROVISION FOR MAN'S SIN. HE DIED, ROSE, AND IS THE ONLY WAY TO GOD (*Romans 5:8, 1 Corinthians 15:3-5, John 14:6*).

LAW IV WE MUST INDIVIDUALLY RECEIVE CHRIST AS LORD OF OUR LIVES—IT IS NOT BY LOTTERY OR COMMITTEE. IT IS DONE BY AN ACT OF THE HEART'S WILL TO TRUST IN A PRAYER OF FAITH (*John 1:12, Ephesians 2:8-9, John 3:1-8, Revelation 3:20*).

Megan's last journal entry was based on the first law—trusting God for his plan because it was good. And I believe that if she were to pray today it would be a prayer that many would come to know, for themselves, her Lord and Savior and that He has a plan and it is always good. She would have wanted her family and friends to know the source of her joy. And then it would be each person's own decision.

Chapter Eleven **Finishing Well**

${M}$egan had traveled a long road —hoping, searching, and trying to reclaim a life she loved and lived fully, but was now relinquishing. She always did her best, even in dying she somehow did that well, but now her body was exhausted. The tension was gone. Her hands were calm without the grip I had learned to cherish, and for the most part she rested.

➡ JULY 5, 2008

While she rested on July 4th, Blair and I joined 56,000 others for the annual Peachtree Road Race. It is a huge parade of all kinds of people—some in wheelchairs, some fit and some not, some in costumes and some dressed like their teammates running for a cause. It is exciting and fun to be part of a sea of people moving down Peachtree, all hoping to finish well.

We all hope to finish well at something. It might be a road race or an advanced degree or recovery from illness. Our hearts cannot live without the hope of finishing well. Brent Curtiss in The Sacred Romance *says it well: "In the trinity of Christian graces—faith, hope, and love—love may be the greatest but hope plays the deciding role...our courage for the journey so often falters because we've lost*

*our hope of heaven—the consummation of our Love Story with God.
No wonder we live like Robinson Crusoe trying to cobble together the
best life we can from the wreckage of this world; we think we're stuck
here forever."* [30]

Hope takes the wreckage of the world and recreates it into something that
extends a hand to others. In Paul Young's book, The Shack, God
explains his role in wreckage. *"Just because I work incredible good
out of unspeakable tragedies does not mean I orchestrate the tragedy.
Don't ever assume that my using something means I caused it or that
I need it to accomplish my purposes. That would only lead you to false
notions about me. Grace doesn't depend on suffering to exist, but when
there is suffering you will find grace in many facets and colors."* [31]

We have found that grace in "facets and colors" as we have traveled this
long-distance road with Megs. God covered her with grace by only
allowing her a little glimpse of fear before He stepped in and shielded
her from full knowledge of what had overtaken her. And it is grace
that keeps all of us going. Scripture reminds us to press on with hope.
I like Peterson's translation of Hebrews 12:2 from The Message,
*"Keep your eyes on Jesus, who both began and finished this race we're
in. Study how he did it. Because he never lost sight of where he was
headed—that exhilarating finish in and with God—he could put up
with anything along the way; cross, shame, whatever. And now he is
there, in the place of honor, right alongside God. When you find yourselves flagging in your faith, go over that story again, item by item,
that long litany of hostility he plowed through. That will shoot adren-
aline into your soul!"*

⌐ JULY 20, 2008 *Give It All Away, Mom*

*Today, Dr. Feelgood sat with our patient while I took some time to work in
the garden. I planted a few more ferns on Megan's Path. But the big
job that I undertook was to uncover the stone steps going up the hill. I
love the uneven, shabby charm of those steps—but the charm was soon
to be lost in overgrowth. Shrubs had quietly crept out from both sides.*

Self-seeding hollies with sharp teeth were shooting up along the edge. Creeping Jenny was twining itself through it all. I became unrelenting in my effort.

I see life somewhat like this stone walk—it can get overrun with obstacles that would trip us, hurt us, sting us, even yank our feet out from under us—almost destroy us. But life is a wonderful gift of God that beckons us onward and upward. We must stay on it and keep the path clear.

I know that Megan's terminal illness is something that happens every day. Someone daily gets bad news. A relationship fails. Harsh words are spilled out, never to be taken back. Financial crises hit. Lethargy consumes. Ego is king. But there is something in all of us—an internal nudging—that beckons us to do something about our personal struggles, to free us from an obstacle-filled life.

The lectionary for this Sunday is the parable of the feeding of the 5,000. When we look beyond the miracle itself and the wonder of it, we find Jesus instructing his disciples to go and find what they could to help remedy the dinner dilemma. And it was not until they found a child with a small lunch that they were able to bring it to Jesus and give it to Him where He blessed it and then gave the directions for feeding the crowd.

Jesus is the one who nudges us, saying, "Go and find what you have and bring it to me." It is when it is given to Him that He can bless it and then feed the multitudes. And for us, the giving of Megan to Jesus, her Savior becomes the "feeding" of so many in ways we will never know, but God knows. God also knows how very hard it is to give up a child. He blesses the offering. The parable says when the meal was over there were leftovers. Jesus said for none of it to be wasted.

Megan holds on to life as we daily give her to Him. Why does she linger so? Many say because her life and beautiful young faith is grabbing hearts and He is "feeding the multitudes" through her life. One of the last sentences she said was in regard to giving some of her teaching resources to her colleagues. It was almost as if she knew she would not need them. And as I gradually let her go, as I give away some of her things to friends, I always see her smile and say with such freedom, "Just give it all away, Mom."

She had become our own Olympic champion as we watched the 2008 Summer Olympics with fascination and appreciation for the feats of the human body. We watched China display their country to the world in proud fashion. Harmony, a word they refer to often describing symbols and ideas of ancient Chinese culture, is based on balancing forces in the universe and it kept returning to my thoughts.

AUGUST 10, 2008 *Going for the Gold*

That word "harmony" caught my attention the other day at my desk. It popped out as I continue to read and try to understand the even more ancient idea of "waiting on God." Yes, my little book is becoming frayed from month after month reviewing the principles laid down in scripture and interpreted by Andrew Murray. He states that "the outer life must be in harmony with the inner; the inner must be the inspiration and the strength for the outer." He says, "It is our God who has made known His way in His Word (Jesus) for our conduct, and invites our confidence for His grace and help in our heart."[32]

We know that every gold medalist looks for the best coach and then practices daily, for years, to do exactly what the coach instructs. I caught a TV clip of a runner training and as he ran, his coach was directly in front of him riding on the back of a truck, instructing him how to adjust and correct as he trained for the race. Learn by doing. What a perfect "training" picture from Psalm 37:34 that says, "Wait on the Lord and keep His ways." Two instructions that offer real harmony— waiting which has to do with worship and attitude; and keeping his ways which is about working it out in our lives—however that looks— as an Olympic athlete or one who is just trying to make it through the day. Don't you know a coach's finest moment must be when the "light" goes on and he sees his athlete understand and carry out a movement or technique that takes him to new heights? Don't you know that God is thrilled with us when we watch Him and do what

*He says? Sometimes it is not exciting. Sometimes we get hurt in the
process. The training can be grueling and seems to never let up. And it
always requires just plain obedience, trusting in the One who "invites
our confidence for His grace and help in our heart."*

*I love Job's comment to his friends as they lamented his struggles. Even as
Job himself questioned, he also declared in 23:10, "But he knows the
way that I take; when he has tested me, I will come forth as gold." That
will be a real victory.*

Megan's days were more erratic now; some where she was alert,
laughing a little with us, eating reasonably, and then days when
we would wonder if she would wake at all. I would sit and watch
the rhythm of her breathing and smile because she was with us. We
could touch her, hug and kiss her, feel the warmth of her beautiful
skin, and savor her elusive presence. She was like the butterflies that
had returned to my garden—flitting around, then very still, disap-
pearing out of sight and then returning again.

•➤ AUGUST 19, 2008 *The Effort of Things to Come*

*The garden somehow carries on in spite of my neglect. The Crape Myrtles
are blooming and the rain has given the vegetables a boost. Some
tomatoes are turning red and small eggplants are forming out of their
lavender blooms. The squash and cucumbers look promising, but the
green beans were too tempting for my resident rabbit. We had high
hopes but the rabbit won.*

*Megan's Path is flourishing. The ferns, hostas, and hydrangeas give prom-
ising hope for a garden path that will only improve over time. Summer
is the time in the garden where we must trust nature to do its thing.
But now we find yellow jackets nesting in several places and will need to
enforce territorial rights if we want to safely enjoy this little path. If I
didn't always find inspiration in the garden, I would give up the effort.*

*But it is in the effort that we find the hope of good things to come, whether
it is in a bloom or a butterfly or death. It is the effort of doing the
best we can do and trusting the rest to God. That's what nature does*

through the seasons—budding, growing, blooming, and then dying until spring comes to revive and restore.

Every day Dr. Feelgood encourages me with our efforts—the routine care of Megan, her meals, schedule, medicine, are somehow never tiring or seem futile. Her few and limited responses inspire all of us with energy to continue. And when some nights I am so very weary of watching the decline, I look at "Megan's wall." There represents hope and faith and love in the form of Godly expressions of the One watching over us all. The crosses, prayers, and scriptures offer me hope and before she goes to sleep, we gather around her as a family and say the prayer that Jesus taught:

OUR FATHER

WHO ART IN HEAVEN

HALLOWED BE THY NAME.

THY KINGDOM COME.

THY WILL BE DONE,

ON EARTH AS IT IS IN HEAVEN.

GIVE US THIS DAY OUR DAILY BREAD.

AND FORGIVE US OUR TRESPASSES,

AS WE FORGIVE THOSE

WHO TRESPASS AGAINST US.

LEAD US NOT INTO TEMPTATION,

BUT DELIVER US FROM EVIL.

FOR THINE IS THE KINGDOM

AND THE POWER

AND THE GLORY

FOREVER.

AMEN

➡ AUGUST 24, 2008 *A Love That Will Not Let Me Go*
I don't mind crying. It is a part of letting go of a beautiful gift—a friendship, a presence of joy in our family that has been rich and alive.

Henri Nouwen says we must let go and in letting go we then can find safety. He says that those who would try to guarantee that their hearts will not be broken end up in some kind of a self-created hell. He then goes on to quote C. S. Lewis who wrote in The Four Loves:

> To love is to be vulnerable...If you want to make sure of keeping your heart intact, you must give your heart to no one, not even to an animal. Wrap it carefully round with hobbies and little luxuries, avoid all entanglements, and lock it up safe in the casket of your selfishness. But in that casket—safe, dark, motionless, airless—it will change. It will not be broken—it will become unbreakable, impenetrable, irredeemable. The only place outside of Heaven where you can be perfectly safe from the danger of love is Hell.[33]

I was reminded of Hell when Mike had me reread a portion of his favorite book, Pilgrim's Progress. *Christian has left his good companions and sets out into the Valley of Humiliation when he "espied a foul fiend," Apollyon, who is the devil.[34] A mighty battle ensues and Christian wins, even though he is wounded terribly. I stopped reading there. Wounded terribly—that would be us, having to fight the "foul fiend" that would work to destroy, discourage, and suffocate us in a mire of personal loss. Christian inspires us to gather all of our strength for the final blow to the enemy and continue on our march to The Celestial City. Wounded terribly, we still win.*

I had to think about this. Satan seeks to destroy all of us every day. While some days are harder than others, it is real freedom (and power) to love (with a breaking heart) and trust in a Creator who will one day wipe away every tear and heal our greatest hurts. As Christian said as he thrust the final wound into Apollyan, "We are more than conquerors through Him who loved us." And I am right back to Jesus Christ, who made himself vulnerable in His own love—even to a cross, taking the sins of the world, conquering evil, and waiting in Heaven, preparing for the day we will meet him face to face. Oh, there is no danger in Heaven's love. It is a love that will never let us go. It is the love that permeates Megan's soul and keeps her peacefully waiting. And it is Heaven's love that will strengthen us for the journey.

◆ AUGUST 30, 2008 *Having it Out with God*

In going through Megan's mail, I opened a letter sent to alumni from the Peabody College at Vanderbilt University. A quote from a Ph.D. student said, "The main theme that runs through everything I'm doing here is being asked to do things and learn things that seem impossible at the time."

I have thought about that quote, and I, too, can say the same thing about everything we are doing here, "being asked to do things and learn things that seem impossible at the time." There are days when it hits me again—we are being asked to let go of one of our children. We are expected to learn how to deal with death—"grief" would be the better choice of words. It seems impossible to be asked to do that.

How do we do it? It is not something any of us want to think about much less actually do. Maybe we have an advantage since we have been in training for a while—we keep trying to focus on the tasks at hand with each day wondering, "Can I handle this?" "Is this the day?"

We read books about others who have been asked to do the impossible. I have decided that books on grieving are sort of like cookbooks. Some you are drawn to and return to time after time. I particularly love The Pat Conroy Cookbook—*it makes me laugh, especially the chapter entitled The Southern Funeral. Others take their spot on the shelf never to be opened. I have voted by the tears called forth during the read and five books on grief sit on my desk reminding me that being asked to do the impossible can stretch, inspire, and challenge. One of them is* Tracks of a Fellow Struggler *by Jonathon Claypool. Claypool lost his daughter to leukemia. After her death, he gave four sermons to his congregation all based on his experience. His story reminds me of our journey.*

In the fourth chapter, he uses the example of Job to offer five possible stages in grief.

STAGE 1 *You experience a state of numbed awareness, merciful but not lasting. Job's friends sat with him in silence for seven days.*

STAGE 2 *Clouds of despair remind you that life is forever changed and you wonder is it really worth it. This is where Job's wife suggests he curse God and die.*

STAGE 3 *You revel in nostalgia, remembering how good life was, or possibly feel guilt.*

STAGE 4 *You feel anger and resentment—this is where Job's friends try to explain his troubles.*

STAGE 5 *Job has it out with God and begins to heal by God giving him what Claypool calls "a new understanding about the past and a fresh vision of the future."* [35]

I think I will reread the book of Job and have it out with God. I need a fresh vision.

Chapter Twelve **Looking Back— Looking Ahead**

I was a creature of habit. After Megan died, I would sit in our bedroom, facing the wall without Megan or her hospital bed. I would look at the collection of art still hanging above the place where she had lived with us. It comforted me to remember how she would seem to find strength gazing at that same wall. And after she was gone I, too, found strength in "He is making all things new," "God cares for you," and "For He will command His angels concerning you to guard you in all ways."

We tried to pick up and resume life—gradually, carefully, and quietly. I was amazed that Blair had the courage to return to college so quickly and Owen resumed a regular work schedule. Routine seemed to help everyone. One morning, standing together at the coffee pot, Dr. Feelgood said quietly, "Would you like to go to the recycling center with me?" He might as well have been asking me to go to Paris. I knew then we would survive. We had set aside our marriage for sixteen months, but after thirty-seven years together, we could still find pleasure in each other—even at the recycling center. We soon returned to the peace and beauty of our church and could feel tender love in the eyes and arms of our family in Christ. We discovered that we could return to the golf course and it became another sanctuary outside where we could be mesmerized by the wonder and orderliness of wildlife and sunsets. Life would continue.

In spite of trying to move forward as different people, I knew that we all felt paralyzed with sorrow and shock that Megan's physical presence was really gone from us. We were all hurting in our own ways and seemed to respect each other's needs for private grief. I knew at some point we would need to redefine "family." Oh, how we loved Megan and missed her terribly. As Jean Valjean sang in the musical, *Les Miserables*, "To have loved another person is to see the face of God."[36]

I was humbled that God continued to give me words to write. It seemed everywhere I turned there was some message, some promise, some affirmation that it would—in time—be well with our souls.

✦ SEPTEMBER 22, 2008 *Stars, Angels, and a White Heron*

God, in His infinite mercy, continues to show His face to us through creation, our spectacular earth, and its abundance. One night, Mike and I looked up at the beautiful pink sunset and there in perfect formation was a huge cloud in the shape of an angel dancing before our eyes. Dr. Cooper wrote and said on the night of September 12th, the stars shown exceptionally bright over the French countryside. She found out later that Megan had died at 8:30 that night. And on the golf course, a white heron circled around us on one particular green. These are gentle reminders that God is near to us, the broken-hearted, and offers comfort and love in rich supply when we seek Him.

I glance up at "Megan's Wall" through my tears and notice one piece of art that she created. It is a painted wooden board—green with blue dots—with her artsy printing that says, "And this is love that we walk in obedience to His commands" 2 John 1:6. And through my shuffling in her journal, I find an index card written from The Message *in Romans 12:1-2, "So here's what I want you to do, God helping you: take your everyday ordinary life—your sleeping, eating, going to work and walking around life—and place it before God as an offering.*

Embracing what God does for you is the best thing that you can do for Him. Don't become so well-adjusted to your culture that you fit in without thinking. Instead fix your attention on God. You'll be changed from the inside out. Readily recognize what He wants from you and quickly respond to it."

I realized that God had changed me from the inside out. I had been pulled from my everyday, ordinary life, and asked to offer my child as an offering. I did not want to do it, but I accepted it with struggling hurt and questioning disbelief, fixing my attention on God. I had chosen early on to trust that God is always faithful and ever present. And in making that decision, I can now see four ways in which he changed me forever.

I am forever changed in that I now believe Philippians 4:13 which says, "I can do all things through Christ who strengthens me." I am not afraid of suffering—or whatever I might be called to do. I may not like it, and will never understand the "whys," but I trust in the One who hears my complaint, knowing that he has a plan and a purpose for all things. I am more serious and intentional, and probably a lot less fun.

I am forever changed because during Megan's illness, God somehow—probably through the prayers of many—revealed Himself, providing me with words that comforted me and others who followed our story. The words chronicled the journey, marked the time, and provided strength. I witnessed personal healing in myself and many others as we watched her leave this life. I am so thankful for this unusual gift.

I am forever changed because though the journey was dark, there was always light. There was always something of beauty that would appear—maybe a friend, maybe a bird or a star, maybe a note, maybe the light in Megan's eyes. There was a presence in our home that was felt and unexplainable, a sense of God's close-up presence and it was real. I still feel it, and I seek it out on my dark days. Light always overcomes the darkness. Don't ever doubt it.

I am forever changed because in my grief I have been taken more closely to the cross of Christ with the realization that God never asked me to do more than what he did in giving up his own son Jesus, on the cross. And on those days that are dark in mystery, I go to Gethsemane and sit with Jesus, and listen to Jesus plead with God, saying, "Could you just take this cup from me? Is there not some other way? Yet, it is not my will, but thy will." [37] And he listens while I ask the same questions and give up my will—again.

I look back and see documented with every journal entry where God was quietly present. He was there throughout, ministering to Megan and to all of us, speaking through the written words. Certainly, now I know God inspired this writing because I could never have done that in my own strength or ability. I was not a writer. When I first started, I was uncertain of my words, and felt inexperienced and vulnerable. As I would reread to edit, I often cried because I knew many of the words were not my own, but God's words ministering to me, helping me to capture my pain in print. I just happened to be a fast typist who could somehow keep up with God's thoughts.

I wrote little about the progression or ugliness of Megan's disease. Instead, I found comfort in nature and wrote about birds, butterflies, gardening, and the weather. I wrote about faith and golf, and Dr. Feelgood, my ever faithful husband. I always seemed to find something to say that would encourage readers, but never too much about my sick child. I know that she would have pointed to something beyond herself and that is what I experienced as I wrote.

Writing became a prayer vigil of sorts. The further Megan slipped away, the faster I wrote. The greater our pain, the faster the words came. I felt stronger after posting an update, like a surge of energy shot through me until the next week. It reminded me of those prayer times when you feel that you and God really connected. Writing marked the time and chronicled the journey. Writing kept me close to God, who was recapturing my heart in the very midst of my grief. Megan's illness and death broke His heart as well because she was so in love with Him. And scripture says that Jesus wept over those He loved. Jesus wept over my child. Jesus ministered to Megan as she left us and went to be with Him. He ministered to my family when often we were at a loss with how to even look at each other. He gave my husband strength and courage to provide stability in the storm, humor when we were faltering, and a father's abounding love for his children. God brought friends, who provided refuge in the storm, alongside my two healthy children and sheltered them in His love. He ministered to me, drawing me close as I wrote, and somehow made my breaking heart available to Him.

The changes that occurred offered challenges then to step out in faith and respond to my pain in ways that could help others. Did not Jesus say to feed sheep? As I moved through the early stages of grief, others set the example for me as they began to give in new ways as a result of our experience. Some organized the sale of daffodils, calling it Daffodils for Hope. The project was started by a garden club and continues to plant bulbs annually in Atlanta, reminding all who admire the multitudes of blooms that we are never without hope. As a thank you for the project created in memory of Megan, I responded by creating note cards of the photographed daffodils and now as I make them I experience healing by knowing others might receive encouragement in their time of need.

A school group organized Megan's Closet, an annual coat drive that supports underprivileged children. I was inspired by their effort and responded by composing a children's story, *Coats for Winter*, to enhance the project and encourage participation. My writing was going in new directions with new possibilities.

I began to discover that we receive blessings even in the worst of suffering. And in my constant searching for some better explanation,

I found a quote by Bishop Mack Stokes of Atlanta. He said, "When amid our suffering and grief, we open our souls to Him in prayer, we receive at least four blessings of importance.

BLESSING 1 Despite our sorrow and grief, we become more profoundly aware of the presence of God. In our depth of weakness and inadequacy, God gives us a vision of the glory and warmth of divine presence. We know the Father will never leave us.

BLESSING 2 We develop a more profound awareness of the height and depth and riches of God's glory and grace. It is one thing to know that God goes with us through life, tragedy, death. It is another to become aware of the vast ranges of God's mysterious love in redeeming, nurturing, empowering us to be used for His glory.

BLESSING 3 We have a new appreciation of the care and support which comes from the fellowship of believers. In church, others suffer with us and the Holy Spirit uses their comforting hands to hold us close.

BLESSING 4 We receive a new vision for service. When we have experienced loss of any kind, the Father opens up a new vision where we can move. God makes us aware where we are to help others." [38]

I can say that through it all, I have been the recipient of each of these blessings.

And as I finish this manuscript, I am thankful that I do have a choice in how I will participate in this great loss. I have a choice in how I will heal and how I will help my family heal as we move forward with hope and trust in the God who came near and waited with us in the miracle of His presence. The good news is that He is still with us every day. My prayer is that I may enlist my suffering and use it continuously until all I can see is an ever-present fresh vision—the glory that God reveals in each one of us through prayer, His Word, and those who abide in Him. And may we all abide in Him.

Soli Deo Gloria!

Further Reading

Death Be Not Proud by John Gunther
Evidence Not Seen by Darlene Deibler Rose
Fifty Days of Heaven by Randy Alcorn
Gold By Moonlight by Amy Carmichael
Hearing Jesus Speak into Your Sorrow by Nancy Guthrie
Light in My Darkest Night by Catherine Marshall
Markings on the Windowsill by Ronald J. Greer
Psalms of Lament by Ann Weems
Shattered Dreams by Larry Crabb
Tears of God by Benedict J. Groeschel, C.F.R.
The Birds' Christmas Carol by Kate Douglas Wiggin
Tracks of a Fellow Struggler by Jonathon Claypool
When God and Grief Meet by Lynn Eib
When the Heart Waits by Sue Monk Kidd

For more information on Creutzfeldt-Jakob disease, visit
the Creutzfeldt-Jakob Disease Foundation Inc. official web site
http://www.cjdfoundation.org.

Citation Sources

Chapter Five 1 Romans 8:26–27
      2 Job 23:10
      3 Creutzfeldt-Jakob Disease Foundation, cjdfoundation.org

Chapter Six 4 Job 2:10
      5 Thomas Howard, *The Night is Far Spent*
         (San Francisco: Ignatius Press, 2007), 245.
      6 Oswald Chambers, *My Utmost for His Highest, An Updated Edition in Today's Language* (Grand Rapids, MI: Discovery House Publishers, 1963), devotional for November 1.

Chapter Seven 7 Warren Wiersbe, *When Life Falls Apart*
         (Grand Rapids, MI: Baker Publishing Group, 1998).
      8 Civilla Martin, *His Eye is on the Sparrow,* 1905
      9 Galatians 6:2
     10 John 16:33
     11 Romans 1:20
     12 Maltbie D. Babcock, *This Is My Father's World,* 1901
     13 Fanny J. Crosby, *All The Way My Savior Leads Me,* 1875

Chapter Eight 14 Randy Alcorn, *50 Days of Heaven – Reflections That Bring Eternity to Light* (Carol Stream, IL: Tyndale, 2006), 92-93.
     15 Judith Couchman, *A Garden's Promise*
         (Colorado Springs: WaterBrook Press, 1997), 87.
     16 Hebrews 12:1-2
     17 Henri Nouwen, *Turn My Mourning Into Dancing*
         (Nashville: Thomas Nelson, 2001), 89-90.

Chapter Nine 18   Henri Nouwen, *Show Me The Way*
                      (New York: Crossroad, 1992), 76-77.

                    19   Henri Nouwen, *Show Me The Way*
                      (New York: Crossroad, 1992), 138-139.

                    20   John Steinbeck, *The Grapes of Wrath*
                      (New York: Viking Press, 1939), 112.

                    21   Oswald Chambers, *My Utmost for His Highest*
                      (Grand Rapids, MI: Discovery House Publishers, 1963),
                      devotional for April 8.

                    22   *Farther Along*, 1911

Chapter Ten 23   Brent Curtis, *The Sacred Romance*
                      (Nashville: Thomas Nelson, 1997), 3.

                    24   Robert Robinson, *Come Thou Fount of Every Blessing*, 1757.

                    25   J.S. Bach, *Jesu, Joy of Man's Desiring*, 1716.

                    26   Matthew 22:1-14

                    27   Ephesians 5:21-32

                    28   Henri Nouwen, *Turn My Mourning Into Dancing*
                      (Nashville: Thomas Nelson, 2001), 102-103.

                    29   Bill Bright, *The Four Spiritual Laws*
                      (Campus Crusade for Christ, 1952).

Chapter Eleven 30   Brent Curtis, *The Sacred Romance*
                      (Nashville: Thomas Nelson, 1997), 178.

                    31   Paul Young, *The Shack*
                      (Los Angeles: Windblown Media, 2007), 185.

                    32   Andrew Murray, *Waiting on God*
                      (Chicago: Moody Press, 1896), 64.

                    33   Henri Nouwen, *Turn My Mourning Into Dancing*
                      (Nashville: Thomas Nelson, 2001) 26.

                    34   John Bunyan, *The Pilgrim's Progress*
                      (London: James Nisbet).

                    35   John R. Claypool, *Tracks of a Fellow Struggler*
                      (Harrisburg, PA: Morehouse, 1974), 79-83.

Chapter Twelve 36   Alain Boublil and Herbert Kretzmer (Lyricists),
                      Les Miserables (Paris, 1980)

                    37   Luke 22:42

                    38   Mack Stokes, *Talking With God*
                      (Nashville, TN: Abington Press, 1989), 88.

Obituary

Atlanta Journal & Constitution

September 14, 2008

Megan McQueen Gaddis, 27, went to be with the Lord on September 12, 2008 after a long neurological illness. Megan was born in Atlanta on August 10, 1981 where she grew up and graduated from the Westminster Schools. While attending Westminster, she devoted her extra time to service projects at the school and her youth group at Second Ponce de Leon Baptist Church. During junior high, she would volunteer on Saturdays by riding around in a mission van, handing out food and supplies for Atlanta Children's Coalition ministry. Dan Hayes, founder of Atlanta Community Ministries, wrote to Megan during her illness, reminding her that she was a founding volunteer for Creative Hearts, an after-school ministry for Hispanic children in the Lindburgh area. She coordinated with friends the gathering of donated Christmas gifts for over 300 children during high school years. At Westminster, she was awarded the Levy Award for Outstanding Service, The Senior Citizenship Award, and was a class officer her senior year.

She went on graduate from Vanderbilt University where she majored in Child Development and Art History. She was an active member of Reformed University Fellowship and Chi Omega sorority where she devoted her time to raising money for Make a Wish

Foundation. The summers during her years at Vanderbilt, she was a counselor at Kanukuk Camps in Branson, Missouri. During her junior year, she was selected to participate in a summer semester at Focus on the Family Institute in Colorado Springs, Colorado. It was after this experience she changed her focus to education, and returning to Atlanta, earned her Masters of Education at Georgia State University. She taught for two years at Park Street Elementary School in Marietta where she was awarded Outstanding New Teacher her first year in the classroom. Dr. Devonne Harper, who hired Megan as a teacher said, "From the first day I met her, Megan radiated poise, grace and wisdom… well beyond her young age. She was always sensitive to the needs of her students and she was very conscientious about searching for creative ways to better serve them. I often reminisce about my visits to Megan's classroom. She created a warm, engaging learning environment for her students. I have vivid memories of her singing, dancing, reading, and writing with her children. From time to time I see her former students, now first and second graders, and I know Megan would be so proud of how well they are doing. She gave them such a solid foundation!" Megan was a member of Peachtree Road United Methodist Church and attended Buckhead Church where she worked with Middle School students. She was a member of the Young Patrons for the Arts at the High Museum of Atlanta and a member of the Southern Foodways Alliance.

She is survived by her parents, Mr. and Mrs. Michael O. Gaddis of Atlanta, one brother Michael Owen Gaddis, Jr. and one sister, Kathryn Blair Gaddis, both of Atlanta and her paternal grandmother Mrs. Levettia Hicks of Campbellsville, Kentucky and lots of aunts, uncles, and cousins. She will always be remembered as a young woman of many talents and many friends of all ages, but loved most for her joy, her generosity of spirit, and her love of the Lord.

⌒ COLOPHON ⌒

TYPOGRAPHY:
Emigre Tribute, designed by Frank Heine
Emigre Triplex, designed by Zuzana Licko
and Bitstream Freehand 591, designed by Hasank
Chapter ornaments improvised from Emigre Tribute Ornaments,
Adobe Wood Type Ornaments, and Zapf Dingbats

PAPER:
Text: Mohawk Superfine 80 lb text
End Sheets: Mohawk Loop 80 lb cover

BINDING CLOTH:
Arristox B, Fern & Vanilla, by Holliston Mills

PRINTING & BINDING BY
Thomson Shore, Dexter, Michigan

DESIGNED BY
David Laufer, Atlanta, Georgia

*Table by
Megan*